family handyman

HANDY HINTS

A Family Handyman Book

Dated ISBN: 978-1-62145-847-0
Undated ISBN: 978-1-62145-848-7
Dated component number: 119100106H
Undated component number: 119100108H

We are committed to both the quality of our products and the service we provide to
our customers. We value your comments, so please feel free to contact us at
TMBBookTeam@TrustedMediaBrands.com.

Text, photography and illustrations for *Family Handyman Handy Hints* are
based on articles previously published in *Family Handyman* magazine
(familyhandyman.com).

Consultant on page 93: Reed's Sales & Services, St. Paul, MN

PHOTOGRAPHY AND ILLUSTRATION CREDITS
30 John Hana; **65, 169, 193** Frank Rohrbach III;
83 Ramon Moreno; **96** Rich Gonzalez; **124** Greg Carroll;
127 Judy Hoppe; **172** Pete Simpson; **179** Mike Murdock;
192 Mike Peterson; **196, 199** *br* Masterfile; **201, 202** Trevor Johnston;
223 David Radtke
Getty Images: Chapter openers/hexagon pattern carduus; **69** Johner Images; **200**
joannawnuk**; 220** David Papazian

All other photographs by Tom Fenenga, Mike Krivit, Bill Zuehlke, and Katie Synold

A NOTE TO OUR READERS

PRINTED IN THE UNITED STATES OF AMERICA
1 3 5 7 9 10 8 6 4 2

SAFETY FIRST—ALWAYS!

Tackling home improvement projects and repairs can be endlessly rewarding. But as most of us know, with the rewards come risks. DIYers use chain saws, climb ladders and tear into walls that can contain big and hazardous surprises.

The good news is, armed with the right knowledge, tools and procedures, homeowners can minimize risk. As you go about your projects and repairs, stay alert for these hazards:

ALUMINUM WIRING

Aluminum wiring, installed in about 7 million homes between 1965 and 1973, requires special techniques and materials to make safe connections. This wiring is dull gray, not the dull orange characteristic of copper. Hire a licensed electrician certified to work with it. For more information, go to cpsc.gov and search for "aluminum wiring."

SPONTANEOUS COMBUSTION

Rags saturated with oil finishes like Danish oil and linseed oil, and oil-based paints and stains can spontaneously combust if left bunched up. Always dry them outdoors, spread out loosely. When the oil has thoroughly dried, you can safely throw them in the trash.

VISION AND HEARING PROTECTION

Safety glasses or goggles should be worn whenever you're working on DIY projects that involve chemicals, dust and anything that could shatter or chip off and hit your eye. Sounds louder than 80 decibels (dB) are considered potentially dangerous. Sound levels from a lawn mower can be 90 dB, and shop tools and chain saws can be 90 to 100 dB.

LEAD PAINT

If your home was built before 1979, it may contain lead paint, which is a serious health hazard, especially for children age 6 and under. Take precautions when you scrape or remove it. Contact your public health department for detailed safety information or call 800-424-LEAD (5323) to receive an information pamphlet. Or visit epa.gov/lead.

BURIED UTILITIES

A few days before you dig in your yard, have your underground water, gas and electrical lines marked. Just call 811 or go to call811.com.

SMOKE AND CARBON MONOXIDE (CO) ALARMS

The risk of dying in reported home structure fires is cut in half in homes with working smoke alarms. Test your smoke alarms every month, replace batteries as necessary and replace units that are more than 10 years old. As you make your home more energy-efficient and airtight, existing ducts and chimneys can't always successfully vent combustion gases, including potentially deadly carbon monoxide (CO). Install a UL-listed CO detector, and test your CO and smoke alarms at the same time.

FIVE-GALLON BUCKETS AND WINDOW COVERING CORDS

Anywhere from 10 to 40 children a year drown in 5-gallon buckets, according to the U.S. Consumer Products Safety Commission. Always store them upside down and store those containing liquid with the covers securely snapped.

According to Parents for Window Blind Safety, hundreds of children in the United States are injured every year after becoming entangled in looped window treatment cords. For more information, visit pfwbs.org.

WORKING UP HIGH

If you have to get up on your roof to do a repair or installation, always install roof brackets and wear a roof harness.

ASBESTOS

Texture sprayed on ceilings before 1978, adhesives and tiles for vinyl and asphalt floors before 1980, and vermiculite insulation (with gray granules) all may contain asbestos. Other building materials made between 1940 and 1980 could also contain asbestos. If you suspect that materials you're removing or working around contain asbestos, contact your health department or visit epa.gov/asbestos for information.

CONTENTS

CHAPTER 1

CLEANING

De-Stink Your Fridge

Lost power can leave a stinky mess in your fridge and freezer. Start by removing the food and wiping everything with a disinfecting cleaning spray. Next, work on all the nooks and crannies inside the freezer. The biggest culprits? The shelf supports. Remove and clean behind them with detergent and disinfectant to get rid of any crud. If they're permanently attached, soak them with cleaning spray. Then stuff the shelves with newspaper and place charcoal briquettes in the lowest drawer or shelf. Finally, replace the old newspaper and charcoal with fresh stuff every day for about a week, or until the smell is gone.

STAINLESS STEEL SINK SAVER

Before you plan to replace your scratched, stained and etched stainless steel kitchen sink, try this trick to extend its life. Give the sink a rubdown with 400-grit extra-fine sandpaper wetted with vegetable oil. Make sure you move the sandpaper in the same direction as the original polishing lines.

SWINGING TRASH

Tired of trash ending up on the floor of your kitchen cabinet instead of in the wastebasket? Here's a simple solution to make filling (and emptying) the basket a breeze. Screw two wire shelf anchor clips to the inside of the door and place the lip of the wastebasket right on the hooks. Not only is it easy to use but there's no more trash on the cabinet floor!

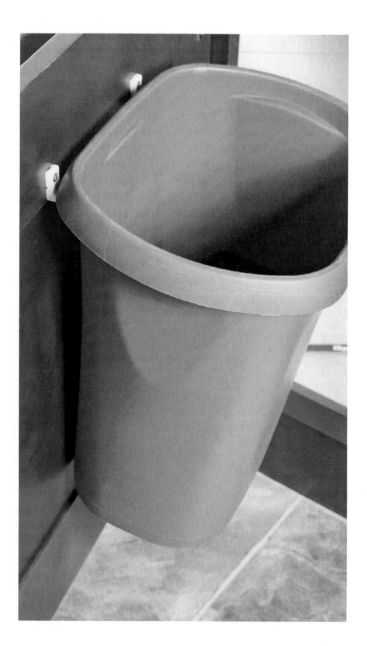

Grease-Free Vent Hood Filter

There are several ways to degrease a vent hood filter, such as running it through the dishwasher or spraying and cleaning it with grease-cutting household cleaners. But none of these methods work as well as a trip to the auto parts store. Pick up a water-based degreaser, and fill your sink with hot water and the degreaser. Drop in the filter, let the degreaser do all the work and rinse it off. You'll have a sparkling clean filter in just a few minutes. If your filter is larger than the sink, clean half of the filter at a time, as shown below.

Clean Sweep

To make sweeping a breeze, modify your dustpan to fit a shop vacuum's floor fitting. Then attach the fitting to the dustpan with a hose clamp.

Hose clamp

GARBAGE BAG HOLDER-UPPER

Tired of the garbage bag slipping down into the trash can? Cut out the middle of the lid with a utility knife and snap the outer rim over the bag to keep it in place. This works great for recycling, but not so great for stinky stuff!

Lid rim

MIX YOUR OWN WINDOW CLEANER

Most professional window washers don't buy window cleaner. They make their own by mixing a teaspoon of dishwashing liquid with a few gallons of water. That's it. You can then pour it into a spray bottle for indoor work. For outside windows, get yourself a combination sponge/squeegee and dip it right in the bucket of cleaner.

Ladder-Free Ceiling Cleaner

Need to clean your high ceilings? Here's a great way to tackle this job without having to balance on a ladder. Start with a paint pad on an extension handle. Spray cleaner onto the pad and wash the spot. Then wipe the area with a clean cloth over the painting pad. The square shape of the pad also helps to reach into corners.

Rust Stain Removal

Throw away the scouring powder and pick up a bottle of resin cleaner used for water softeners (about $11 at home centers). Just douse a foam brush with the cleaner and rub it onto the rust. Usually the rust will disappear in a few minutes, but long-term stubborn rust buildup may take a few treatments. You can even use this cleaner on acrylic spas. You really don't want to scour those! Just try it first on a small area to make sure it doesn't damage the surface.

RESCUE YOUR CARPET FROM PET ACCIDENTS

Scooping up cat or dog poop with paper towels or rags can actually force it into the carpet. Instead, use a putty knife and dustpan to scrape it up as shown.

FUR FILTER FOR DOG BATHING

Washing Fido at home is a lot less expensive than going to a groomer but can cause a fur-clogged drain in the bathtub or shower. To prevent this, use a mesh-type scrub pad. In a shower, clip the pad to the drain plate with a bobby pin. In a bathtub, wedge two pads under the stopper from two sides. The pads will catch fur but let water flow through.

Scrub pad

Trash-Can Vacuum Breaker

Nature abhors a vacuum. And you understand that feeling when you try to pull a full plastic bag out of a trash can. The bag forms an airtight seal inside the container, creating a vacuum as you try to lift the bag. Break the vacuum and save your back by drilling a 1/2-in. hole in the can. Drill through the side, near the bottom. If you drill through the bottom, disgusting garbage liquids can leak out.

1/2" hole

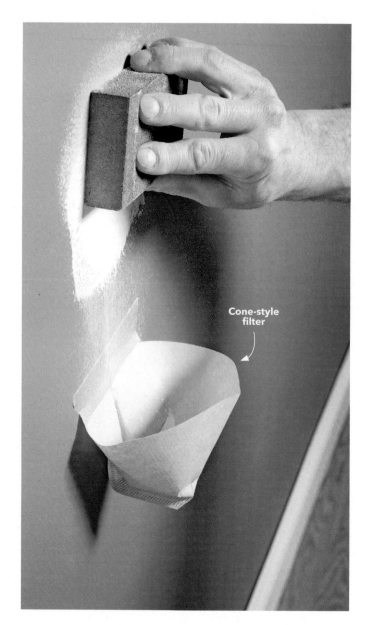

Cone-style filter

Tidier Wall Drilling

Don't feel like dragging out the vacuum to clean up a small pile of drywall or plaster dust after a minor wall repair? A cone-style coffee filter makes a great dust catcher. Tape the seam side to the wall beneath your repair and the filter will automatically hang wide open and catch the dust. Then just toss the filter when you're done.

GREAT GROUT HAZE CLEANER

If you are tiling a backsplash or floor, here's a simple tip: Use a scrap of carpet to clean off the grout haze and buff the tiles to a shine in one easy step. The carpet fibers are slightly more abrasive than a sponge or cotton rag but not abrasive enough to scratch the tiles. They just remove the grout haze quickly with minimal elbow grease. If you don't have a clean carpet scrap handy, check at a home center—most have small samples available for free.

Carpet scrap

SHOVELING YOUR SHOP

Sure, you can buy long-handled dustpans to make cleanup easier on your back, but a child's snow shovel does the job just as well and costs much less. You can get a kiddie shovel for less than $10 at home centers and discount stores.

Ventilated Shop Vacuum Attachment

The floor attachments for shop vacuums can get suctioned to the floor, making it difficult to pick up debris. Attachments for newer models have risers on their bottom edges to improve performance. For an older attachment without risers, there's an easy fix: With a hacksaw, cut 1/4-in.-deep notches every inch or so along the rim. Now the attachment will slide around easily and clean much more effectively.

Minimize Concrete Dust

If you've ever mixed bagged concrete, you know what a dusty job it is. You end up wearing and inhaling a lot of the concrete mix! Have a helper hold a shop vacuum hose close to the top of the bucket. The vacuum catches a lot of the dust before it goes airborne.

SIMPLE PUTTY KNIFE CLEANING

When you're stripping furniture, use this easy method for getting all the goo off your putty knife. Make some slits in the side of a cardboard box and just pull your knife through the slits. All the goo will drop off into the box. The stripping chemicals can be combustible, so make sure you let the goo dry thoroughly before disposing of it.

EXTEND THE LIFE OF YOUR FRIDGE

IF YOU'RE LIKE MOST OTHER HOMEOWNERS, cleaning the refrigerator condenser coil is at the bottom of even your low-priority list. You know that a dirty coil wastes electricity, but the $6 annual electrical savings probably isn't enough to motivate you. Need a better reason? You're killing your fridge. A dirty condenser coil makes the compressor run longer and hotter, and that dramatically reduces its life span. With some refrigerators costing $1,000 or more, it's time to get with the program and clean the beast. I'll show you how to do the job in half the time by blowing the coil clean, rather than brushing it.

You'll need an air compressor, a wand-style compressed air gun, a vacuum cleaner with a hose, a box fan, a pleated furnace filter (not the cheap fiberglass kind), nut drivers and a paintbrush.

Start by converting your box fan into a dust collector. Tape the furnace filter onto the intake side of the box fan. Seal off any open grille area on the fan with masking tape so all the air has to get pulled through the filter. Then pull the refrigerator away from the wall and unplug it. Seal the sides of the refrigerator to the floor with masking tape to prevent dust from blowing out sideways. Next, remove the back access panel fasteners and grille with a nut driver and set the grille aside. Unsnap the grille in the front of the fridge to expose the condenser coil.

Set the fan/filter unit behind the fridge and turn it on to its highest speed. Then aim the compressed air gun at a corner of the condenser coil and blow it clean in bursts **(Photo 1)**. Continue cleaning until no more dust comes out the back of the fridge. Let the box fan run for a while to remove any airborne dust. Then shut it down and toss the filter.

Move to the back of the fridge and clean the condenser fan blades **(Photo 2)**. Then suck up any remaining dust and cobwebs from the back side. Reinstall the access panel, plug in the fridge and push it back into place.

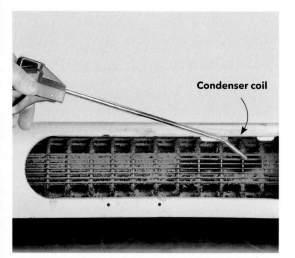

Condenser coil

1. BLOW THE DUST OFF THE COIL

Tape a furnace filter to the intake side of a box fan and place it close to the rear of the fridge. Then shoot one-second bursts of compressed air into the condenser coil. Allow time between each burst so the fan can collect the dust cloud from the back of the fridge. Then move the wand to the next dirty section and do some more quick bursts.

Condenser fan

Access panel

2. BRUSH AND VACUUM

Brush the dust off the condenser fan blades with an old paintbrush and suck up all the crud with the vacuum cleaner hose. Then clean the access panel grille and compressor.

Protect Refrigerator Electronics

Even if your refrigerator doesn't have a jumbo jet-style control panel on the door, it most likely has a solid-state circuit board inside. That means it's at risk for damage caused by power surges coming from within the house or the power lines outside. And those electronics can cost nearly as much as the original fridge.

Protect the electronics by replacing your receptacle with a surge protection receptacle (one choice is the Leviton No. 5380-IGI 20-amp Surge Suppressor Receptacle). Turn off the power. Check to make sure it's off with a voltage sniffer. Then replace the existing receptacle with the surge suppressor as shown below. Tuck all the wires back into the box, secure the receptacle and cover plate, and turn on the power. Test by plugging in the fridge.

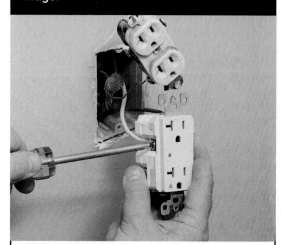

INSTALL A SURGE SUPPRESSOR RECEPTACLE

Disconnect the wires from the existing receptacle and move them to the corresponding screws on the surge receptacle. Black wires connect to brass-colored screws, white to silver screws. Connect the ground wire to the green screw.

CHAPTER 2

ORGANIZATION

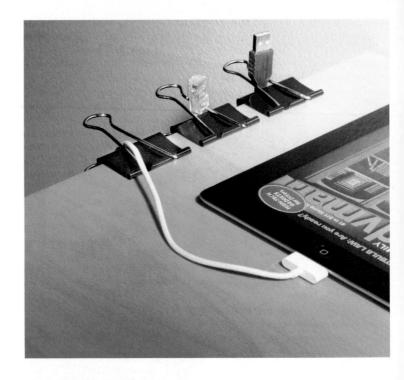

BINDER-CLIP CABLE CATCHER

If you haven't run across this particular cable-organizing tip yet, it's time you take note. It's dirt simple and pure genius. Clamp a binder clip to the edge of your desk to holster USB cables. No more cables slipping behind your desk into the dusty darkness below.

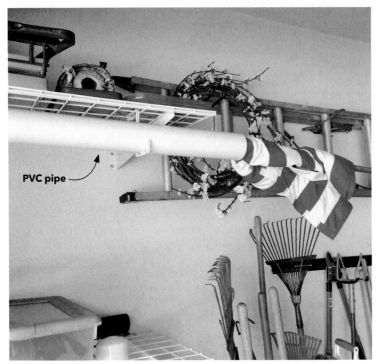

PVC pipe

EASY FLAG STORAGE

Storing an American flag in a dusty corner of the garage doesn't feel very respectful. To keep it clean and protected while it's put away, store it in a length of PVC drainpipe hung on the wall. The pole-mounted flag slides inside the pipe, which can be loosely capped on each end.

Ornament Ho-Ho-Holder

Here's a nifty way to store Christmas ornaments using clear plastic tubs (with lids), wooden dowels and rubber leg tips from the home center. Drill two holes in each end of the tubs, insert the dowels through the holes and cap the dowels with the rubber tips to keep the dowels in place. Store items like Christmas tree skirts in the bottom and hang ornaments from the dowels. Now it's really easy to see which ornaments are in each tub!

Ready-To-Go Hangers

If clothes are hung up immediately from the dryer, they stay fairly wrinkle-free. To keep hangers handy, install a towel bar right above the dryer under the cabinets. When the clothes are dry, just grab a hanger and hang them right away instead of stuffing them into a laundry basket.

Tension rod

EXTRA SHOWER STORAGE

Need more space to hang storage bins in the shower? Next time you're at the home center, grab a shower curtain tension rod. Install it near the wall of your shower for 6 ft. of bin-hanging space!

TURN-OF-THE-CENTURY OFFICE SUPPLY HOLDER

Screw hose clamps to a board and mount it on the wall in your home office. Secure mason jars in the hose clamps to create clever storage for office supplies such as stamps, paper clips and string. The clear jars let you immediately see where everything is. This is also a great idea for bathrooms and workshops.

Storage Above Windows and Doors

The empty wall space above doors and windows is organizational gold! Hang a shelf there and use it for bathroom towels, toiletries, books, files, tablecloths—the list is endless.

Vacuum Gear

It seems as if the vacuum cleaner always ends up in one closet, the vacuum cleaner bags in another, and the attachments get shoved in a corner or spread all over the floor. Here's a simple tip that will keep everything together and out from underfoot: Screw a hook to the door of your storage closet and hang a mesh or cloth bag on it. You can store all your vacuum cleaner bags and attachments in one place, and the bag lets you carry everything you need from room to room or up and down the stairs in one trip.

SLIDING TIE AND BELT RACK

Keep your closet neat and organized with this handy rack for ties and belts. You can build a simple one from plywood, dowels and a full-extension 12-in. drawer slide. Drill holes in the wood and pound in the dowels (use a dab of glue if they're loose). Attach the drawer slide to the side of a closet shelf or the wall, and the rack to the slide. If you need even more hanging room, add a block of wood to the side of your shelves to offset the slide, and attach dowels to both sides of the rack. The drawer slides come in pairs, so you might as well make another one for your spouse to use for more belts and scarves.

TOO MANY CLOTHES FOR YOUR CLOSET

Who doesn't need more space to hang all their clothes? Here's an easy way to add space for hanging clothes that don't require a tall space. Hang a second clothes rod from the upper rod with lightweight chains. Attach the chains to screw eyes directly or use S-hooks or carabiners. Carabiners make adjusting the height of the extra rod a snap. This system works well in kids' closets since kids grow quickly (and their clothes grow along with them). But it also works well in an adult's closet—you can hang pants on one rod and shirts on the other.

Instant Laundry Room Cubbies

If you don't have cabinets or shelves in your laundry room, here's a simple solution to create a wall of cubbies using inexpensive plastic crates from a discount store ($5 each). Screw them to wall studs using a fender washer in the upper corner of each crate for extra strength. The crates hold a lot of supplies and prevent drippy items from spilling on the washer or dryer.

Toilet Paper Shelf

Need more shelving in your tiny bathroom? Turn a deep "shadow box" picture frame from a craft store (about $12) into a bathroom shelf. Cover the frame with a couple of coats of white enamel paint, and when dry, hang it around the toilet paper holder. It gives you two convenient shelves for small items and looks like a high-end shelf.

DIY Drawer Dividers

Here's an easy way to make your own inexpensive drawer organizers. Attach thin strips of adhesive-backed foam weather stripping to the inside of your drawer (either to the sides or to the front and back, depending on which way you want your drawer divided). Then set 1/4-in. plywood strips into the drawer with the ends pressed against the weather stripping. Add as many dividers as you need, and voilà—a perfectly organized drawer.

Foam weather stripping

PUT A LAZY SUSAN NEXT TO YOUR STOVE

Having to reach into a cabinet or drawer for frequently used oils, vinegars and sauces is a recipe for frustration. Instead, store them on an attractive lazy Susan on the counter next to your stove. Top the lazy Susan with a plastic mat for easy cleaning. No more frantic searches in the middle of cooking dinner (and all those condiments in full view will make you look like an expert cook!).

KITCHEN TRAY IN THE BATHROOM

A silverware drawer insert works just as well in the bathroom as it does in the kitchen. The various compartments are perfect for organizing toothbrushes, toothpaste, razors, clippers, lip balm and more.

PVC Knife Holders

Carrying kitchen knives safely for picnics and camping trips is challenging. You can make knife containers simply out of PVC pipe and caps. Glue the cap on one end and mark the unglued cap with an "X." That way you'll always know which end to open.

Roll of garbage bags

Handy Garbage Bag Storage

Here's a good old janitors' tip that a lot of readers have shared. Store your replacement garbage bags right in the bottom of your garbage can. When the old bag is full, the new one is right where you need it. (This tip works best for garbage cans that are unlikely to hold wet, messy stuff.)

SPACE-SAVING HOSE STORAGE

If you have a small yard, don't waste precious real estate on a bulky hose reel. Pound a 4-ft. length of galvanized steel pipe ($7 at home centers) into the ground, and coil up to 50 ft. of hose around it. Attach a hose nozzle that can hang from the end of the pipe.

SCREW BIT MAGNET

It's common for a box of screws to include a bit—with star or Torx heads, for example. But it can be annoying if you can't find that bit when you need it. So next time you buy a box of screws, store them in a glass jar and glue a magnet to the inside of the lid. The magnet can hold the bit, and you won't have to dump out all the screws to find it.

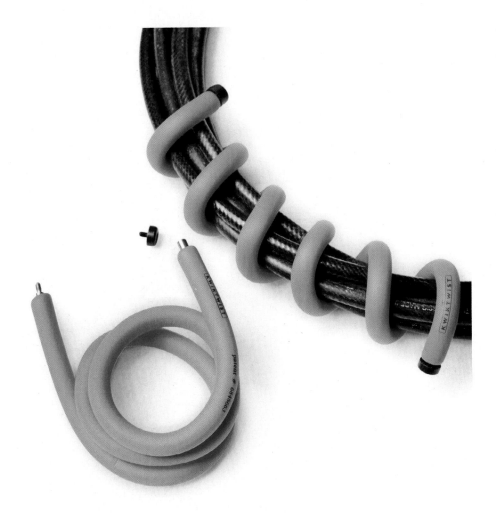

A Better Hose Wrangler

There are lots of different products for tying up cords and hoses, including bungees, hook-and-loop straps and cable ties. They all work pretty well. But consider foam ties, which are unique for a couple of reasons. Unlike bungees, they won't stretch or scratch things, they're longer (32 in.) than most cable ties, and the ends are threaded. You can connect several of them to bundle up or hang larger objects like lawn chairs, bikes and ladders. Each tie holds up to 100 lbs.

Storing Fishing Rods

This is for all you fishing addicts out there. When the season ends and the gear comes out of the truck, where do you store your rods? You can buy a fancy storage rack or make one of your own, but either way you're giving up precious wall space until spring. Here's a quick solution: Screw short sections of wire shelving to your ceiling. If the handles don't fit, just clip out some of the wire with bolt cutters. Your rods will be safely out of the way until your next fishing trip.

PIPE CLAMP HOLDER

A good place to store bar and pipe clamps is right under your workbench. Buy lengths of 3-in.-diameter PVC or ABS pipe, cut out a notch to fit each clamp jaw and then fasten each pipe under your workbench. Just slide the clamps into the pipes—they'll always be right where you need them.

3" PVC pipe

Access holes

Drill 1/2" hole to fasten each pipe

PATIO CUSHIONS AND CAMPING GEAR

Extra-large Ziploc bags (about $2 each at home centers and online) are great for storing camping gear, patio cushions and out-of-season clothes. Here's a slick trick for getting all the air out of the bag before you seal it: Put your items inside and push out all the air you can by hand. Then seal the bag but leave an opening large enough to fit a drinking straw. Use the straw to suck out the remaining air and then finish sealing the bag.

EXTRA ELECTRICAL CORDS

Ever wish you had one more garage wall to hang stuff on? Well, you do. Your garage door is a perfect place to store lightweight items like extension cords. (Yes, they'll stay put when the door opens and closes.) Install screw eyes diagonally about 8 in. apart and thread bungee cords (with the ends cut off) through the eyes. Now you have a perfect bungee "corral" to hold your extra extension cords.

What's in the Garden Sprayer?

Do you use your garden sprayer for pesticides, herbicides and fertilizers. To remember which solution is in it, pick up some key chain tags at the hardware store. Add the product info to the tags and clip the corresponding one to the sprayer. Problem solved! The model isn't wearing protective gloves; be sure you do!

Key chain tag

Tight-Space Garage Storage

Some garages are too narrow for large shelving systems, but here's a great way to store a lot of stuff in very little space. Hang several wire racks on the wall—the same kind you'd use in the pantry. They hold a lot of products, and since they hug the wall, they don't get in the way.

CUSTOM CORD WRAPS

Make your own cord wraps using old bungee cords and synthetic wine corks. Drill two holes in the cork, thread any length bungee cord through the holes and tie off the ends. They are very lightweight and work great for securing air hoses and other unruly items.

EASY ID SYSTEM FOR FASTENERS

Tired of opening every drawer in your plastic storage bin to find the screw or fastener you're looking for? Keep only a certain item in each drawer, then hot-glue one item to the drawer front. Now you can instantly find exactly what you need.

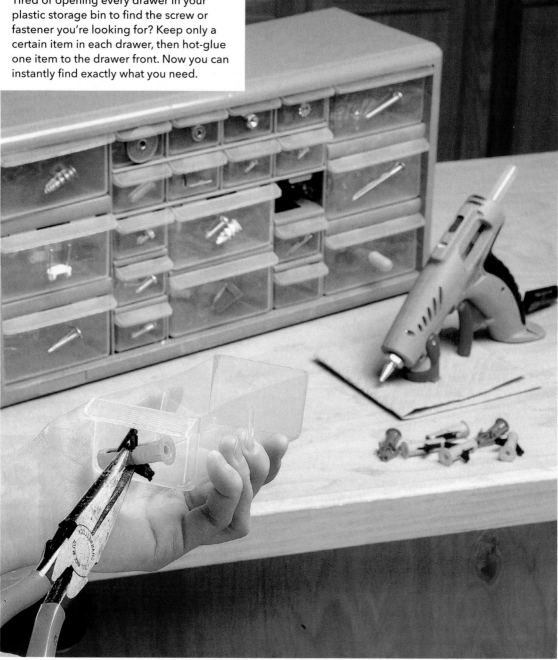

Wet Paintbrush Storage

Here's a way to keep your paintbrush fresh while you take a break in the middle of painting. Snip the corner of a zippered reusable bag. Then slide your paintbrush inside the bag, handle first, and zip it closed. The paintbrush won't dry out and the mess will stay inside the bag.

Memory Saver

It's almost impossible to keep all the different wrench and socket sizes for your lawn mower, snow blower and leaf blower straight—not to mention the different tire pressures for bikes, cars and trucks. No need to remember all these stats! Just keep an ongoing list of these items (and lots more) taped to the inside top of your toolbox. When it comes time to do the job, this list is right where you need it—with the tools! Now you won't spend extra time trying to remember what goes with what.

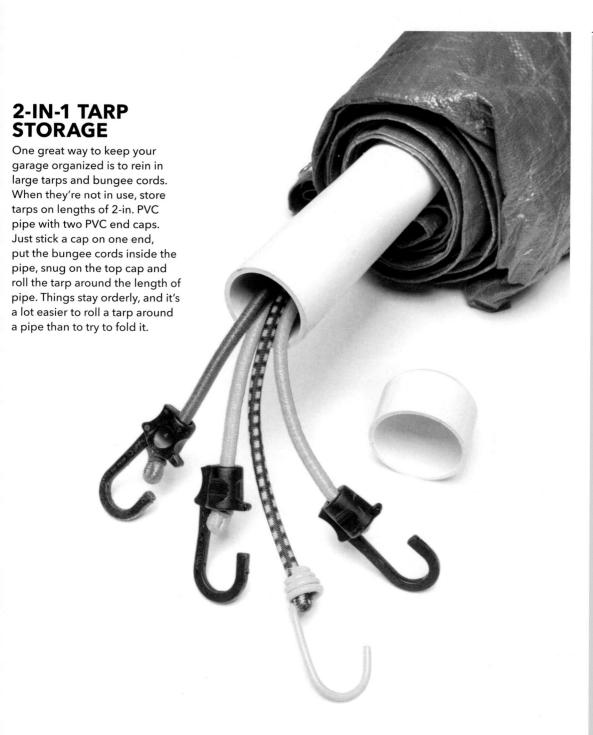

2-IN-1 TARP STORAGE

One great way to keep your garage organized is to rein in large tarps and bungee cords. When they're not in use, store tarps on lengths of 2-in. PVC pipe with two PVC end caps. Just stick a cap on one end, put the bungee cords inside the pipe, snug on the top cap and roll the tarp around the length of pipe. Things stay orderly, and it's a lot easier to roll a tarp around a pipe than to try to fold it.

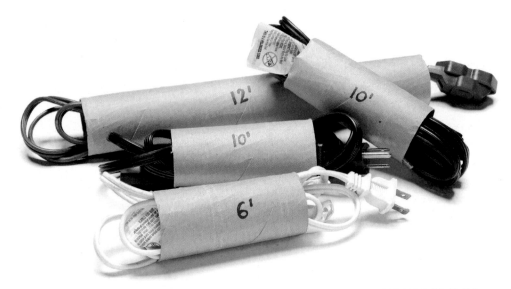

EXTENSION CORD STORAGE

Give this old-fashioned but very effective way to keep extension cords organized a try. Slide them into toilet paper and paper towel tubes. Before placing into the drawer, write the length of each cord on the tube. That way, you can spot the right cord for the job instantly, and it's also a good way to recycle all those paper tubes.

GARDEN HOSE REEL CORD HOLDER

Here's a neat way to store air hoses or extension cords without the fuss of knots and kinks. Use a garden hose reel. It stores 200 ft. of hose or cord, and it's easy to transport in the back of a truck or trailer.

Garage Ceiling Bin Storage

If you store stuff in big plastic storage bins and need a place to put them, how about the garage ceiling? Screw 2x2s to the ceiling framing with 3-1/2-in. screws spaced every 2 ft. Use the bins as a guide for spacing the 2x2s. The lips on the bins should just brush against the 2x2s when you're sliding the bins into place. Then center and screw 1x4s to the 2x2s with 2-in. screws. The garage ceiling is a perfect place to store light and medium-weight seasonal items like holiday decorations and camping gear.

3-1/2" screw

2" screw

1x4

2x2

ORGANIZATION IN YOUR GARAGE

Camping Gear

Beach Stuff

Holiday Dec

Flexible T-Rack Storage

Here's a hanging T-rack that combines two different types of storage space. One side is a typical U-shaped rack for storing pipe and other items that might roll off. The other side is a horizontal rack that allows you to load and unload lumber and molding from the side, instead of from the ends. This is very useful in garages and basements where space is tight.

WRENCH WITHIN REACH

When you change the blades on your band saw, do you adjust the thrust bearings and guides with an Allen wrench? Instead of having to look for one every time, stick an Allen wrench to the steel housing with a rare earth magnet (neodymium) about the size of a jacket button. Now it's always handy!

BIN TOWER

Tons of easy-access storage—and more space to hang stuff!

CUT UP THE PLYWOOD We used BC sanded pine plywood for this project. The holes and blemishes on the "B" side are filled and make for a good painting surface. It's not furniture grade, but it's priced right and works well for garage projects like this one. Rip all the sheets down to 23-3/4 in. If you don't own a table saw, use a straightedge and make your cuts with a circular saw (for more info, search "cut straight" at familyhandyman.com).

Once all the sheets have been ripped down, cut the tops, bottoms and shelves to 18-in. lengths. If you're using a circular saw, save time by clamping two 8-ft. strips together and cut two at a time. Some home centers will make your cuts for you.

PAINT THE PARTS BEFORE ASSEMBLY Finishing the cut components before you assemble them will save you a bunch of time, but before you start painting, figure out which edges need to be painted—the back edges of the sides don't and only the front edges of the shelves do. Configure all the parts so the best edges face out. Mark an "X" with a pencil on all the edges that needed paint. Some of the edges will have voids in the wood that will need to be filled (**Photo 1**).

We applied a product called MH Ready Patch (found at most home centers). It's easy to work with and dries fast, but it's not stainable, so you may want to find a more traditional wood filler if you plan to stain your project. Make a couple of passes with 100-grit sandpaper before you paint. Cover the wood with a paint/primer in one (**Photo 2**). If you choose a traditional wood primer, have the store tint it close to the final color.

ASSEMBLE THE TOWERS We used an 18-gauge brad nailer with 1-1/2-in. brads to quickly attach the shelves to the sides, three brads on each side. If you don't have a brad nailer, that's OK; you can assemble everything with screws only. Cut a piece of plywood 18-5/16 in. wide to align the shelves (**Photo 3**). The spacer board may scuff up the paint a little bit, but you can touch it up when you paint over your fastener holes after everything is all put together. Arrange the sides so the good surface faces out. The good surface on the bottom four shelves should face up, and the top two should face down. That way, you'll see the nicer finish from almost any angle.

1 Figure out which edge will be exposed on each part, and fill any voids in the plywood. When the filler dries, sand the edge with 100-grit sandpaper.

2 Save yourself a ton of time by painting or staining the individual components of this project before you assemble them.

After everything is nailed together, come back and install two 2-in. trim-head screws into each shelf (use three if you're not using brads). Wood glue won't hold well because of the painted sides, so we were a bit concerned about the strength of the tower. We built a small mock-up of one shelf using the same fastening pattern and it held up well.

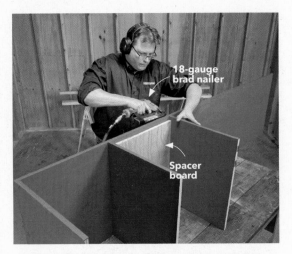

18-gauge
brad nailer

Spacer
board

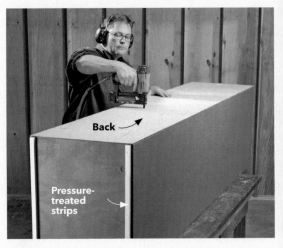

Back

Pressure-
treated
strips

3 Tack the shelves into position with a brad nailer. Then strengthen each connection with 2-in. trim-head screws. A plywood spacer lets you position parts perfectly without measuring.

4 Use the factory-cut edges of the plywood back to square up your project. Start on the top or bottom, and then work your way up the side. Check for square before finishing it off. Reinforce it all with screws.

INSTALL THE BOTTOM STRIPS Plywood will eventually rot if it's sitting directly on a concrete floor. To avoid this, we ripped 5/8-in. strips from a 1x2 pressure-treated board and installed them on the bottom (**Photo 4**). Four square blocks would also keep the plywood off the floor, but we wanted to avoid any space where screws, washers or any other little objects could get lost. We inset the strips about 3/8 in. and nailed them on with 1-1/2-in. brads.

FASTEN THE BACK Use the 1/4-in. plywood to square up the unit (**Photo 4**). Fasten the two factory-cut edges of the plywood to the back first using 1-in. brads. Nail the short side, and then the long side, aligning the edges as you go. Don't install a whole bunch of brads until you know everything is square. Flip the piece over and check for square using a framing square or by measuring from inside corner to inside corner on a couple of different openings—if the measurements are the same, you should be good to go. Finish fastening the back with brads spaced every 8 in. or so, then reinforce it with one 2-in. trim-head screw in the center of each shelf and five screws on each side.

SCREW IT TO THE WALL In many garages, the concrete floor slopes toward the overhead door. That means you'll probably have to shim the bottom to get the bin tower to sit straight and tight up against the wall. We're a big fan of composite shims: They don't compress as much as wood, they break off cleanly, and they never rot. Set the first tower against the wall and shim the front until it sits tight against the wall. Use a level to check for plumb while you shim the low side. Insert at least four shims on the side and three on the front. Go back and snug up the front shims.

Once the tower is plumb, screw it to the wall studs with 2-in. screws. Make sure each tower is fastened to at least one stud. Since tipping is a concern, install a few screws near the top; you'll only need screws down low if you need to draw the tower tight to the wall.

Mark all the shims, and pull them out one at a time. Cut them down to size and replace them. We ran a small bead of clear silicone around the bottom of ours to hold the shims in place. If the towers ever get moved, the silicone will be easy to scrape off the floor. Finally, go get started organizing.

FIGURE A
BIN TOWER

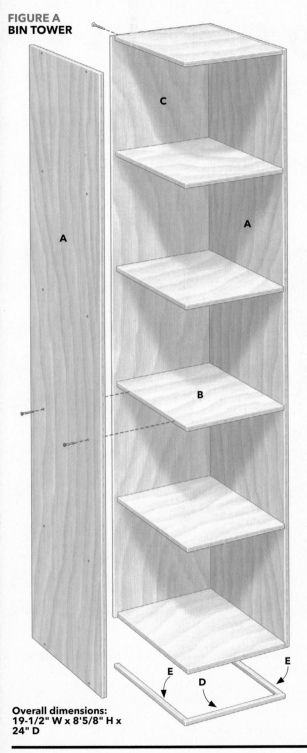

Overall dimensions:
19-1/2" W x 8'5/8" H x
24" D

WHAT IT TAKES

SKILL LEVEL
Beginner to intermediate

TIME
One weekend

TOOLS NEEDED
Table saw/circular saw, drill, 18-gauge brad nailer (optional)

CUTTING LIST (FOR THREE TOWERS)

KEY	QTY.	SIZE & DESCRIPTION
A	6	23-3/4" x 96 x 3/4" BC sanded pine plywood (sides)
B	18	18" x 23-3/4" x 3/4" BC sanded pine plywood (shelves)
C	3	19-1/2" x 96" x 1/4" sanded pine plywood (backs)
D	3	5/8" x 3/4" x 18-3/4" pressure-treated lumber (front bottom strip)
E	6	5/8" x 3/4" x 22-7/8" pressure-treated lumber (side bottom strip)

MATERIALS LIST (FOR THREE TOWERS)

ITEM	QTY.
4' x 8' x 3/4" BC sanded plywood	5
4' x 8' x 1/4" underlayment plywood	2
1" 18-gauge brads	1
1-1/2" 18-gauge brads	
2" trim head screws	
Can of wood filler or patching compound	
Gallon of paint/primer	

FIGURE B
CUTTING DIAGRAMS FOR 3/4" PLYWOOD

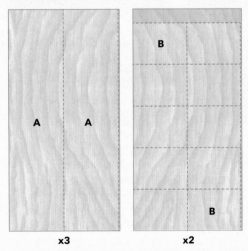

HOW TO GET RID OF ANYTHING

DIY jobs generate junk. Here are some slick disposal tips.

WHETHER YOU'RE CLEANING OUT YOUR BASEMENT, replacing an old appliance or tackling a big remodeling job, getting rid of the old stuff is a pain. To help you out, we surveyed our staff and Field Editors for ideas and discovered tons of great tips and strategies for clearing out everything from cast-iron bathtubs to old sidewalks.

"Free" Makes Junk Vanish

You know the old saying "One man's trash is another man's treasure." The simplest way to get rid of stuff is to just put it on the curb with a "free" sign. When Gary Wentz, one of our editors, knocked down a stone retaining wall, he put a "free stone" sign on the curb. People were practically fighting over the rubble, and 12 tons of stone vanished in one afternoon. But don't be surprised if something reappears. Field Editor Cory Cochran put a freezer by the road with a sign that read "free–broke." It was gone the next day. Then a few days later, Cory found it back in his yard. Maybe he should have added "no returns" to the sign.

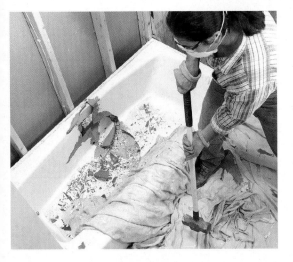

Break Up a Cast-Iron Tub

Some things are just so heavy to move in one piece that you shouldn't unless you absolutely have to. A cast-iron bathtub is one of them. The trick is to break it up with a sledge. But be careful! Cast-iron shrapnel is sharp and dangerous. Cover the tub with a blanket or drop cloth, and be sure to wear long sleeves, safety glasses and hearing protection. Don't expect the tub to break easily on the first swing. You may have to hit the same spot repeatedly to get a crack started. It's hard work, but at least you won't break your back trying to lift the tub in one piece. This trick works for cast-iron radiators and pipes too.

Cut It Up Fast with a Ferrous-Metal Blade

Here's the blade we used to cut up the water heater. It's engineered to cut any mild steel, so when you're done cutting up your old water heater or refrigerator, you can cut angle iron, rebar, metal conduit or threaded rod, to name a few items. You'll find ferrous-metal cutting blades at home centers and hardware stores for about $40.

Cut a Water Heater in Half ⌃

It's a lot easier to move a water heater in two pieces—especially if it has 50 lbs. of sediment in the bottom—and it's surprisingly easy to cut one in half. You could use a recip saw, but a circular saw with a ferrous-metal cutting blade is faster. Be sure to wear goggles or a face shield, hearing protection and long sleeves. Many appliances can be cut; just be careful not to cut through refrigerant tubing or glass.

Give It Away Online

Even if you think no one would want the item, list it in the "free" category on a website. You'd be amazed at what people will take. Our Field Editors have gotten rid of all kinds of junk this way: half-rotten fence planks and worn-out appliances. Here's a list of websites where you can place listings to sell, give away or trade your stuff, plus find information about recycling and safe disposal: craigslist.org, earth911.com, freecycle.org, greenergadgets.org, and usell.com.

Turn Waste Wood into Mulch ⌃

Here's an ingenious idea from Field Editor Tom Berg. After making sure the nails were removed, he ran 2,200 sq. ft. of siding through a wood chipper to make a mountain of great-smelling cedar mulch for his gardens. He saved a ton in trash container fees and had loads of free mulch to boot. You could do the same with pine or any other soft wood, but the mulch will decompose quicker than cedar.

Get Money for Metal

You can get money for almost any kind of scrap metal. You won't get much for steel (currently about 35¢ per pound), but that's better than paying to get rid of it. And other metals are worth a lot more: about $3.65 per lb. for copper and $2.65 per lb. for bronze. You can even pull circuit boards out of electronic equipment and turn them in for bucks.

Dry Out Your Old Paint

If you have a bunch of almost-empty cans of latex paint and don't want to take them to the recycling center, here's a tip: Spread a sheet of plastic—painter's plastic is cheap and readily available at home centers and hardware stores—in an out-of-the way spot and dump a thin layer of paint on it to dry. When the liquid has evaporated, bundle it up and throw it in the trash.

« Buy a Bagster Bag

If you have too much junk to fit in your trash can but not enough to warrant renting a 10- or 20-yard trash container, then a Bagster bag is the answer. Buy the green poly bag at a home center or hardware store, fill it up and call the company for a pickup. The bag holds 3 cubic yards or up to 3,300 lbs. of debris. The Bagster bag costs $29.95. When you're done with it, you'll be charged a flat rate of $80 to $160 to have it picked up, depending on collection costs in your area. Find out more at thebagster.com.

Recycle a Sidewalk ⌄

Why spend a fortune hauling away old concrete when you can build a wall or path with it? Several of our Field Editors used old concrete from torn-out sidewalks and driveways to build paths, patios and walls. For walls, stack it like flat stones with the broken side facing out. For paths or patios, you can lay the broken pieces of concrete like flagstones and then plant a creeping ground cover or pour gravel between them.

Excess Dirt Is an Opportunity ⌃

Digging a hole for a pond or fountain? You can save yourself time and money by turning the extra dirt into a landscaping feature. Here we piled the dirt along the back of the pond to create an earth berm. Covered with plants, the berm made a perfect backdrop for the pond.

Disassemble Your Old Box Spring

Field Editor Andrew Pitonyak stripped the fabric and padding from his box spring and left the metal springs on the curb for the local scrap collector to pick up. He saved the $20 cost of getting rid of the box spring and helped the environment by recycling the metal.

CHAPTER 3

MAINTENANCE

DISHWASHER RACK REPAIR

Dishwasher rack tines sometimes break off or lose the protective coating at the tips and then you get rust spots on your dishes. New racks cost about $80 (and up). But you can fix yours in less than an hour and for about $13. Buy a bottle of vinyl repair paint and a package of replacement tips to match your rack color (from any appliance parts store or fixture-fix.com). Cut off the rusted tips with a rotary tool and cutoff wheel. Then retip the tines (**photo inset**).

To patch a rusted area around a broken tine, first clean off the rust (**photo bottom**).

Chair rung

Cheater's Chair Fix

When you don't have hours to spend disassembling and regluing a rickety chair, try this simple technique. Drill pilot holes and drive trim head screws through the bottom of the rungs and into the legs. Be sure to use screws that are long enough to run through the rungs and well into the legs. One reader used this technique and their chair is still sturdy after 15 years!

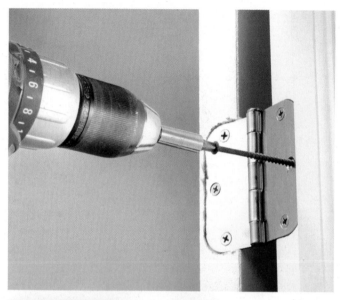

Fix a Sagging, Self-Closing Door

Here's a simple way to repair your door if it slowly "creeps" closed. If it swings freely, the door or wall is out of plumb and will require more draconian fixes, which aren't covered here.

Check the gap at the top of the door. If it's wider at the doorknob side, remove the center screw at the top hinge and replace it with a 3-in. screw (**photo top**). The screw will pull the jamb and door tighter to the framing and hopefully fix the problem.

If the door still creeps closed (but less so), go to the "Kleenex box" shimming technique (**photo bottom**). Put one shim behind the middle hinge and two shims behind the bottom hinge.

Stripper blade

REMOVE VINYL FLOORING THE EASY WAY

No need to spend hours on your knees, ripping up an old floor. Here's the fasted way to remove vinyl flooring. Rent a power floor scraper, which rents for about $40 for four hours.

Start by scoring the vinyl (**photo bottom**). Next, adjust the angle on the floor scraper until it pulls up vinyl without gouging the subfloor. Turn it on and let 'er rip (**photo top**).

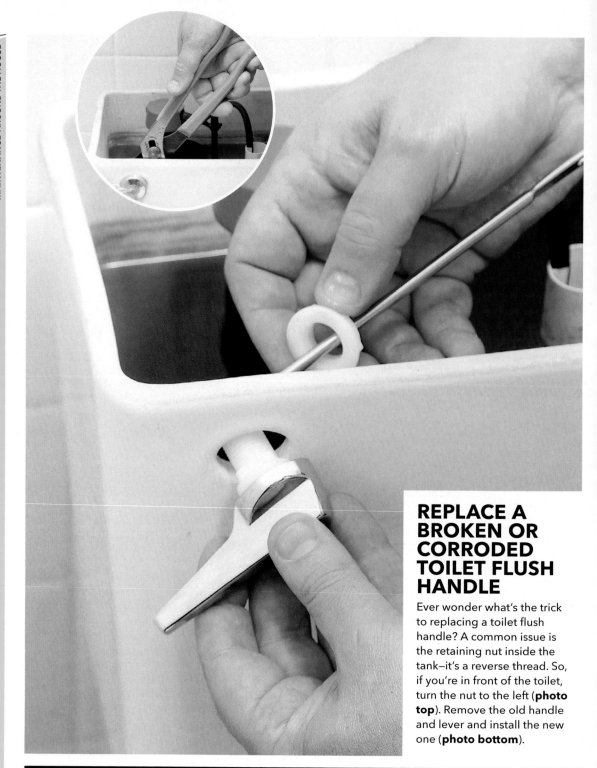

REPLACE A BROKEN OR CORRODED TOILET FLUSH HANDLE

Ever wonder what's the trick to replacing a toilet flush handle? A common issue is the retaining nut inside the tank—it's a reverse thread. So, if you're in front of the toilet, turn the nut to the left (**photo top**). Remove the old handle and lever and install the new one (**photo bottom**).

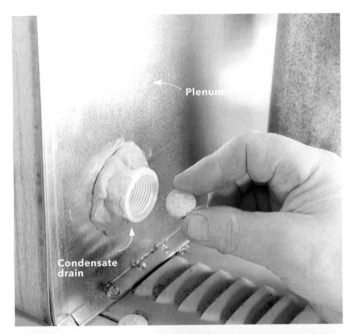

Plenum

Condensate drain

Fix a Clogged Condensate Drain

If water is puddling near the furnace with the A/C running, you have a clogged condensate drain tube. And it contains bacteria that can form slime and clog the condensate pan drain tube. Here's how to prevent this: First, remove the drain tube and fitting from your A/C condensate pan. Toss them. Next, buy a package of slime-preventing tablets. Follow the package dosing directions and insert the tablets right into the drain pan (**photo top**).

Next, buy a 3/4-in. MIPT barb fitting, a small coil of 3/4-in. I.D. vinyl tubing, and several tubing straps. Then install the larger tubing (**photo bottom**). The pan tabs will reduce slime formation, and the larger-diameter tubing will enable faster condensation flow.

Tilt toward jamb

Lock in place

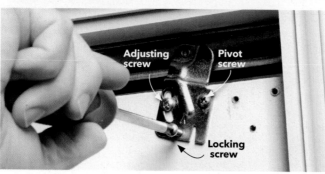

Adjusting screw

Pivot screw

Locking screw

Adjust Bypass Closet Doors

There's no reason to put up with sticking bypass closet doors, or doors that have uneven gaps against the jambs—especially since they're so easy to fix. Usually the mounting bracket screws have loosened up, making the door sag and rub against the carpet or floor.

First, square the door by push the door against the jamb and lock it in place with shims at both corners.

Next, you'll have to work from inside the closet, so get a flashlight and screwdrivers. Start by pushing one door closed against the jamb. Hold it against the jamb while you adjust the brackets as shown. Do the same on the other door. If the screw holes are stripped, just move the bracket over a few inches and remount it.

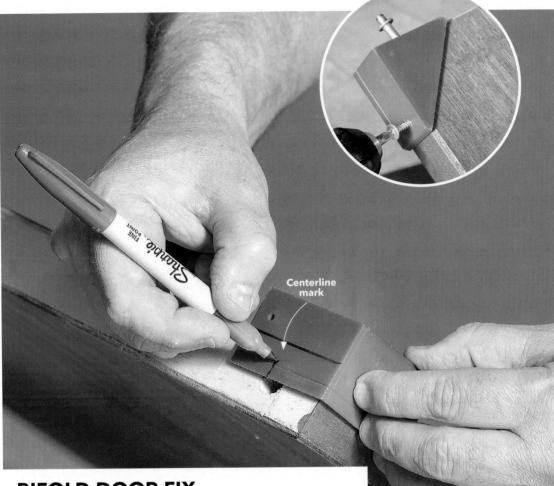

Centerline
mark

BIFOLD DOOR FIX

Slam a bifold door too many times and you can split the wood
where the top and bottom anchors and pivot pins sit. Then the
door either sags or falls out of the track. You can fix the problem
permanently by installing corner braces. Buy a corner-brace kit at
a home center or from maintenanceengineeringspecialties.com
($6 for three braces). Take the old anchor/pivot pins to the store
to match up to new ones.

Start by marking the anchor pin hole location on the new
brace. Hold the brace along the door edge with the triangu-
lar area on the back of the door. Then mark the anchor/pivot
pin hold centerlines (**photo bottom**). Slide the brace onto the
corner and secure it at the top with one screw. Drill a hole for the
anchor/pivot pin. Tap in the new anchor/pivot pin and secre the
jamb side of the brace with one additional screw (**photo top**).
Then install the door.

FIX AN OVERSIZE ELECTRICAL BOX CUTOUT

We've all done it—cut the electrical box opening too large. Sure, you can cover it with a jumbo electrical plate, but it can look pretty odd, especially if other boxes are nearby. Instead of squishing joint compound into the gap (it'll always crack), try this fix. First prepare the gap and fill it with compound **(photo top)**. Then apply joint tape and additional mud coats **(photo bottom)**.

Tape

Foam a Loose Showerhead

No time to do a major repair? A wobbly shower arm should be repaired by cutting into the wall and refastening the plumbing. But for a quick fix, shield the wall with plastic and inject a few shots of expanding foam. The foam encases the pipes in the wall and eliminates the wobble.

Remove Metal Scratches from Porcelain

You're supposed to use a closet auger to remove toilet clogs. But many DIYers don't have one and use a regular snake. Sure, it works, but it can also leave metal scratches on the bowl. If that happens to you, don't freak out. Just pick up a pumice stone from any home center. Wet the stone and keep it wet while you gently scrub the marks. Don't scrub too hard or you'll scratch the porcelain. And don't be surprised if the stone wears away quickly—that's normal.

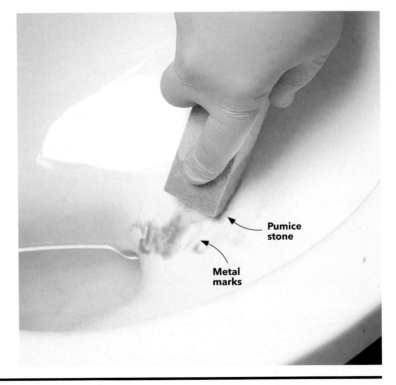

Pumice stone

Metal marks

Restore Free Flow to a Faucet

If your kitchen or bathroom faucet loses pressure because of a dirty aerator screen, cleaning a screen is an easy job. Start by closing the drain plug (so you don't drop parts down the drain). Then remove the aerator, using a rag or masking tape so you don't mar the finish with your pliers.

To remove the sand and other deposits, soak the aerator in vinegar, then scrub it with a toothbrush. This usually solves the problem. If you have to disassemble the aerator to clean it, lay out the parts in the order you removed them so you can reassemble them correctly.

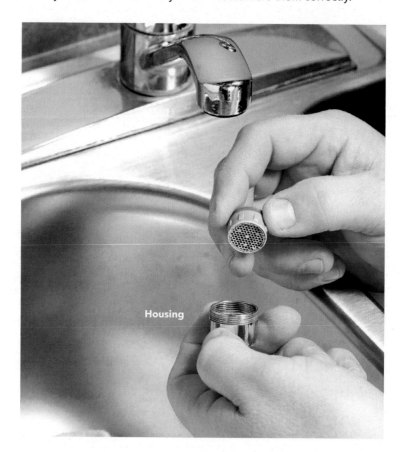

Housing

BETTER TUB CAULKING

Here's an old plumber's trick to try before you caulk the seal between your tub and the tile wall. Step inside the tub. If it flexes or you feel any movement at all, fill the tub with water and stand in it while you caulk (make sure to use silicone). Let the caulk dry before you drain the water. The weight of the water (and you) will settle the tub slightly downward or outward. This will help the caulk seal last longer because it won't stretch when you use the tub.

FIX A SQUEAKY FAUCET

Outdoor frost-proof faucets eventually develop a squeal when you turn the handle (**photo top**). The brass stem threads are rubbing against the brass threads in the housing. If there's a shutoff valve for the faucet, close it. Otherwise, shut off the main valve. To get rid of the squeal, apply a dollop of plumber's grease (**photo bottom**).

No Kinks, No Damage

Ever have the hose of your pressure washer dancing all over the driveway from the pulses generated by the pump, and as a result, almost wearing through in several spots? To preserve the hose, go to the auto supply store and buy some inexpensive black split-wire loom. It slips over the high-pressure hose quite nicely, and protects the hose from wear. Plus, it prevents kinking, the most common cause of hose damage.

Self-Draining Dehumidifier

If you forget to empty the tank on your dehumidifier, it'll either overflow or shut off. That defeats the whole purpose of running a dehumidifier in damp areas. If you don't have a floor drain in the basement, buy a condensate pump ($40 to $100 at home centers) and tubing and rig it to your dehumidifier. Then run the tubing up to the ceiling, through the joist areas and down to the laundry tub. Now the dehumidifier can run full time, and you'll never need to empty the tank or worry about it shutting off.

From dehumidifier

To laundry tub

Condensate pump

SILENCE A SQUEAKY FLOOR

To fix a squeaky floor under carpet, locate the floor joists with a stud finder, then drive in a trim head screw through the carpet, pad and subfloor, and right into the floor joist.

Be sure the top inch of the screw doesn't have threads or the subfloor won't suck down tight to the joist. Trim screws are ideal because screws with larger heads pull down and pucker the carpet. If that happens, back out the screw and drive it back down. Keep adding screws until the squeak stops.

REPAIR A CABINET-HINGE SCREW HOLE

Cabinets made from particleboard are great for some uses. But particleboard has a major weakness—it doesn't hold screw threads very well, and the hinge can rip the screw right out of the cabinet wall. Don't worry; the fix is easy and cheap. You'll need a bottle of wood glue, a 1/2-in. drill bit and a package of 1/2-in.-diameter hardwood plugs.

Start by removing the hinge screws on the cabinet and flipping the hinge out of your way. If the accident pulled out a large chunk of the particleboard, glue it back into place and let the glue set up before proceeding with the rest of the repair. Drill out the stripped screw hole to accept the plug. Next, fill the hole with wood glue and install the plug (**photo top**). Then drill a pilot hole (**photo bottom**) and install the new screw—you're all set.

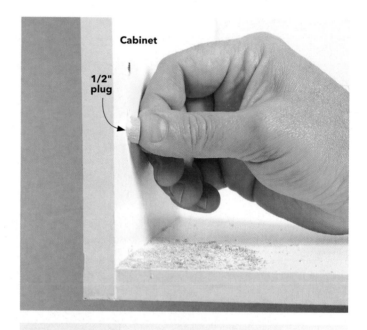

Cabinet

1/2" plug

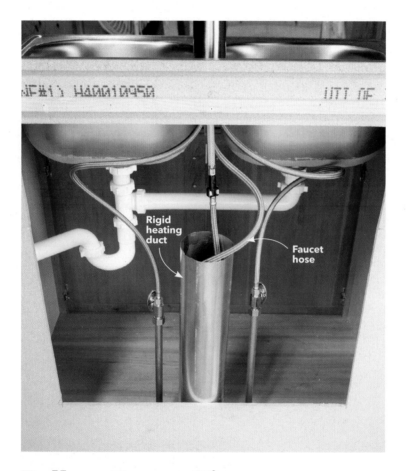

Rigid
heating
duct

Faucet
hose

Pullout Faucet Fix

Does your pullout faucet hose gets wrapped around things under the sink? They can interfere with shutoff valves and other important features of the sink. Here's a simple solution to the problem. Purchase a 2-ft. piece of 4-in. rigid heating duct. Prop the duct up under the sink and push the faucet hose down into the duct. Now the hose should slide freely without getting wrapped around anything. If the duct won't stay upright, screw it to a block of wood that's screwed to the bottom of the cabinet.

Construction
adhesive

Rolled-up
cardboard

Reuse Drywall Cutouts

Whenever you need to make an electrical repair inside a finished wall,
cut an opening with a hole saw and save the round plug. Later, when
you're ready to patch the hole, glue a piece of rolled-up cardboard to
the back of the plug using construction adhesive.

Then glue the other end of the tube to the drywall on the other side
of the wall. Cut the cardboard tube slightly shorter than the depth
of the wall studs so that the plug sits just below the surface of the
drywall. Then finish off the patch with some joint compound.

FIXING A SCREWY ELECTRICAL BOX

If you're dealing with a loose receptacle inside a plastic electrical box, the screw holes in the box may be stripped. To fix the problem, slip small zip ties into the stripped holes, and you'll be able to tighten the screws until snug.

Zip tie

WHEELBARROW TIRE FIX

Isn't it annoying to pull your wheelbarrow out from winter storage to find flat tire? Often, a nail is the most likely culprit.

In about 10 minutes, you can fix flat tires with a one-shot bottle of tire sealant (**photo top**). At the hardware or auto parts store, determine how much sealant you'll need by checking your tire size on the installation chart on the bottle.

To fix a punctured tire (and avoid future ones) with tire sealant. Remove the plastic valve cap, deflate the tire, then, using the core removal wrench, unscrew and remove the valve stem core (**photo bottom**). Connect the clear plastic tube to the bottle of tire sealant, press the tube's connector tightly to the valve stem and squirt the required volume of sealant into the tire.

Fix Tubeless Tire Leaks

Got a garden tractor tire that's always low and you can't find a puncture? The easiest solution is to install an inner tube and put an end to deflated tires. Write down the tire size and buy the same size tube.

Start by cutting off the old valve stem with a side cutters or utility knife. Next, break the bead **(photo top).** Slide a large screwdriver or pry bar down the center of the wheel and clamp it in a vise. Then pry the bead off the wheel **(photo middle).**

Rotate the inner tube so the valve stem lines up with the valve stem hole in the wheel. Tuck the inner tube inside the tire and pull the valve stem through the hole. Secure the valve stem with a spring clamp. Then pry the tire bead back onto the wheel and reinflate **(photo bottom).**

Engine Markup

Use a permanent marker to write the exact oil blend needed for your two-cycle engine on any clean surface of the tool. It'll save you from running to the file cabinet to find your manual or grabbing the wrong mix.

QUICK, NO-MESS FUNNEL

Every time you add oil, coolant or windshield washer fluid to your car, you spill a little, right? Keep a supply of unwaxed paper cups in the garage to use as funnels. When needed, just punch a hole in a cup bottom and throw it away when you're done. No mess. They're perfect for filling mowers, chain saws or any container with a small opening.

Unwaxed paper cup with hole in bottom

MOTOR OIL SMART SPOUT

Have a hard time pouring motor oil into your snow blower engine without spilling? Head to the kitchen for a solution. Use a spout common for olive oil and vinegar bottles—it screws right onto motor oil bottles. Now you can pour without a mess—but don't return it to the kitchen!

Small-Engine Oil Dispenser

Want a handy, no-mess way to add oil to small engines? Use a dishwashing detergent squeeze bottle with a push-pull plastic top. Rinse and dry the bottle thoroughly and fill it with oil. You can hold it at any angle and aim the spout into those hard-to-reach holes. Pull open the top and give the bottle a squeeze to add just what you need.

Flexible Funnel Keeps Things Clean

If you do your own oil changes, you need this formable funnel. It bends, molds and flexes so you can channel the oil right into your drain pan. But it's not limited to auto repair. You can use it for plumbing repairs too. The funnel comes in four sizes. Best of all, you can flatten it and keep it right in your toolbox.

LAWN MOWER OIL-CHANGE TIP

Most late-model lawn mowers don't come with a bottom oil drain plug. So you have to tip the entire lawn mower on its side and drain the oil out of the oil filler tube at the top of the engine. Before you do that, unscrew the gas cap and lay a plastic bag over the gas tank opening. Then screw on the cap. The bag prevents gas from leaking out of the gas cap vent. Here's another tip: Always tilt the mower on the side opposite the air cleaner so you don't drain gas out of the carburetor at the same time.

Plastic bag

Oil filler tube

FOUR FIXES FOR A NOISY GARAGE DOOR

Give your door the care it needs with these fast fixes

WHEN A GARAGE DOOR MAKES NOISE, it's usually just screaming for a bit of TLC. We'll show you some fixes to quiet down any garage door. And, if you have a tuck-under or attached garage, we'll show you how to reduce the vibrations and noise that transfer to the living space.

Test the noise level by opening the door after each fix and quit when things are quiet enough for you.

Before you get started, go to Home Depot and pick up a Prime Flo garage door lubrication kit for $7. You'll get all the lubricants you need for this job. Also pick up rollers if you need them for Fix #4.

Fix #1 Isolate the Opener

If you have an attached or tuck-under garage and your opener seems loud inside the house, try this step. Mechanically isolate the opener from the garage rafters/trusses with rubber pads. Cut rubber pads out of an old tire, or buy specially made rubber/cork anti-vibration pads. (Four 5-1/2- x 5-1/2- x 3/8-in. pads are $14 at amazon.com. Just search for "anti vibration pads.") You'll be adding about an inch in thickness, so you'll need four longer lag screws and four fender washers.

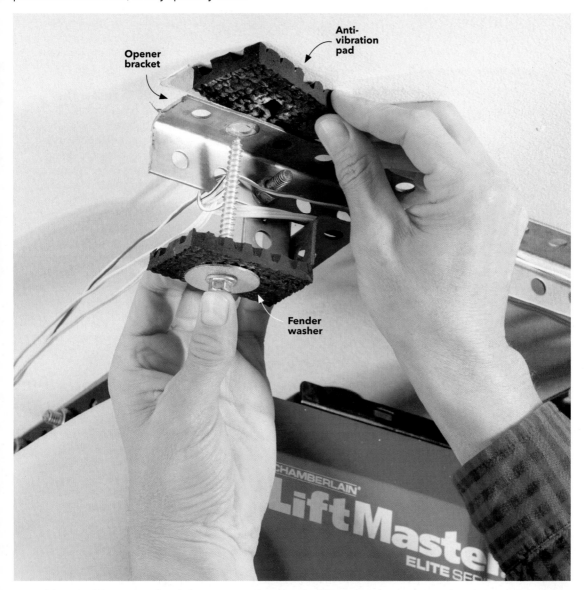

1 Add anti-vibration pads. Slide one anti-vibration pad between the mounting bracket and the ceiling and the second pad under the bracket. Then slip a fender washer onto the new lag screw and drive it into the rafter with a socket wrench or impact driver. Repeat on all four corners of the opener bracket.

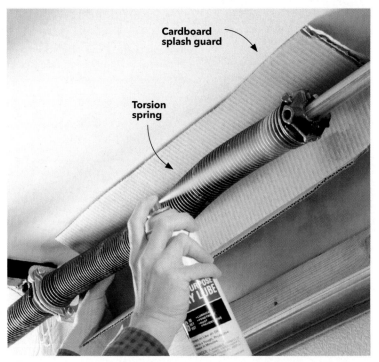

Cardboard
splash guard

Torsion
spring

Fix #2 Lube the Hardware

Next, quiet all the garage door's moving parts with garage door lube spray. It works much better than spray-on oils because it stays in place and dries to a greaselike consistency. The grease also does a better job of quieting moving parts. Repeat this step every six months.

Fix #3 Tighten the Chain and Lube the Opener

A loose garage door opener chain makes loud slapping sounds and causes jerky door movements that smack the rollers against the track. So start by tightening the chain (find the procedure in your owner's manual). If you have a track drive opener, the next step is to lubricate the opener track with grease. If you have a screw drive opener, grease the threads.

2 **Lube everything that moves.** Spray the roller shafts and hinges first. Wipe off the drippy excess. Then slip a piece of cardboard behind the torsion springs and soak them, too.

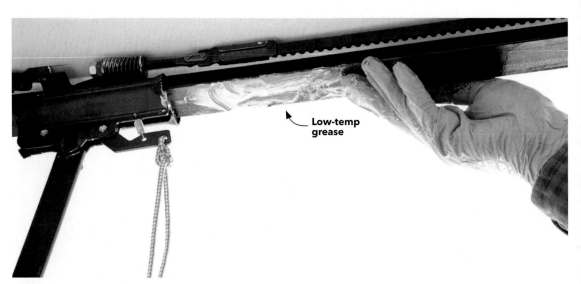

Low-temp
grease

3 **Grease the track.** Squeeze a large dollop of grease onto your gloved hand and wipe it onto the track. Operate the opener several times to spread the grease along the track and into the trolley.

Fix #4 Install Quieter Rollers

If your garage door has steel track rollers, they're part of your noise problem. Buy eight "quiet" nylon rollers. They're equipped with bearings and cost a few bucks more than nylon bearingless rollers or nylon rollers without end caps, but they're quieter, roll smoother and last longer. You can find them at home centers and online at garage-doors-and-parts.com.

Swap out the steel rollers for the new nylon ones (one at a time). If your door uses torsion springs mounted on the header above the door, do NOT attempt to replace the rollers in the two bottom brackets. Those brackets are under constant spring tension and can cause serious injury if you unbolt them. That's a job for a pro.

4 Install new rollers. Remove the hinge retaining nuts and tilt the hinge/bracket toward you. Swap out the rollers and reverse the procedure to reinstall. Then reinstall the nuts and snug them up with a wrench (but don't overtighten).

7 TRICKS TO START A DEAD ENGINE

Before you call for help, try these tips to get revving again

MOST PEOPLE DON'T KEEP a set of mechanic's tools in their trunk. So when you get stranded with a dead engine, you feel pretty helpless. But don't give up right away. Here's a list of tricks you can try, and none of them require tools. They're arranged by symptom, and you've got nothing to lose by trying them. Of course, they won't fix the root problem, but one of them just might get the engine started so you can head to the nearest mechanic to have the problem fixed.

Symptom: Starter Goes "Click"

This can be caused by a weak battery, dirty battery terminals, a worn starter motor or a stuck solenoid. Here are a few tricks to try:

1. CYCLE THE KEY

Turn on the dome light and watch it while you try to start the engine. If the light goes out, it's a sign the battery is really weak—almost dead. To heat up the battery, terminals and starter, try the "key cycling" trick (**photo 1**). But if the dome light stayed bright when you turned the key, move on to the next trick.

2. TAP ON THE BATTERY TERMINALS

There's no way to clean corroded battery terminals when you're stranded without tools. But you can try to move or at least jar the terminals enough to make better contact (**photo 2**).

3. SMACK THE STARTER

If you have access to the starter motor, try smacking it with the tire iron from your car jack. Sometimes, the electrical contacts get stuck and can be freed by tapping on them.

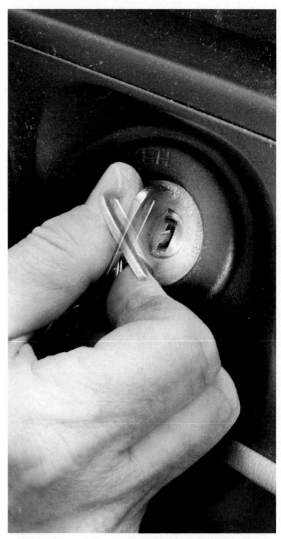

1 **Cycle the key.** Turn the key to the start position repeatedly about 10 times in a row. Stop and wait five minutes. Then try to start the engine.

Your shoe

Battery terminals

2 **Bang terminals with a shoe.** Smack each battery terminal with the heel of a shoe to rotate it slightly around the battery post. Then try starting the engine.

Fuel tank

3 Smack the fuel tank. Hit the bottom of the fuel tank several times with the heel of your shoe. Then try starting the vehicle.

Symptom:
No Click When You
Turn the Key

4. SHIFT THE SHIFTER

With your foot on the brake, move the shift lever to the neutral position and try starting the engine. If that doesn't work, move it back to "Park" and try it again. Moving the shifter sometimes reestablishes electrical contact inside the transmission range selector (also known as the neutral safety switch).

Symptom:
Engine Cranks But
Won't Fire Up

5. SWAP RELAYS

With the radio off, turn the key to the "Run" position and listen for a two-second buzzing sound. That's the fuel pump priming the injection system. If you don't hear any sound, the fuel pump relay may be bad or the pump may be on its last legs. First, find the location of the fuel pump relay in your owner's manual or on the legend of the under-hood fuse box cover. Then locate another relay with the same part number and swap it with the fuel pump (**photo 4**). Try starting the engine afterward. If it still won't fire, beat on the fuel tank with your shoe to jar the fuel pump motor (**photo 3**).

6. UN-FLOOD A FLOODED ENGINE

If you smell gas, the engine is flooded. Press the accelerator pedal to the floor and hold it there while you crank the engine.

7. TRICK THE COMPUTER

A vacuum leak or funky temperature sensor can result in an air/fuel mixture that's too lean to start a cold engine. If you've tried all the other tricks shown here and it still won't start, press the accelerator halfway and try to start the engine. That'll tell the computer to add more fuel.

Relay

4 **Swap relays.** Yank the fuel pump relay straight up. Then align the pins on the replacement relay and push it straight into the socket.

CHAPTER 4

DIY HINTS

HEAVY-DUTY LID TWISTER

Jar openers for food items come in many styles and sizes, but this strap wrench made for oil filters is the best. It gives all the leverage needed and works on lids from 1 to 8 in. in diameter.

Better Cord Connections

Isn't it annoying when your tool stops in the middle of your project because the extension cords disconnected? Next time you connect two extension cords, tie them using an easy overhand knot. This way, the cords will stay connected when you drag them around a job site.

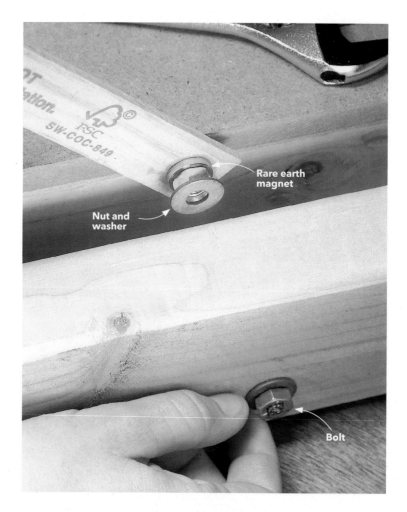

Rare earth
magnet

Nut and
washer

Bolt

Magnetic Stick Trick

In a hard-to-reach area, it can be frustrating to get a nut into place
when you need to thread on a bolt from the other side. Here's a slick
trick. Glue a small rare earth magnet to the end of a paint stir stick,
attach the washer and nut to the magnet and use the stick to hold
them while you thread on the bolt.

SUPER-SEAL PLUNGER

For a better seal and more effective plunging, smear petroleum jelly on the bottom rim of your plunger.

Petroleum jelly

QUICKER FIXTURE MOUNTING

Surface-mounted fixtures come with a layer of foil-faced insulation, which can make it difficult to line up the mounting keyholes with the screws on the electrical box. Using a screwdriver as a guide saves a lot of time and frustration. Slip the screwdriver shaft through the keyhole and stick the tip in the screw head. Slide the fixture over the shaft, rotate the fixture until the second screw comes into view, and then twist the fixture on the screwheads and snug them up.

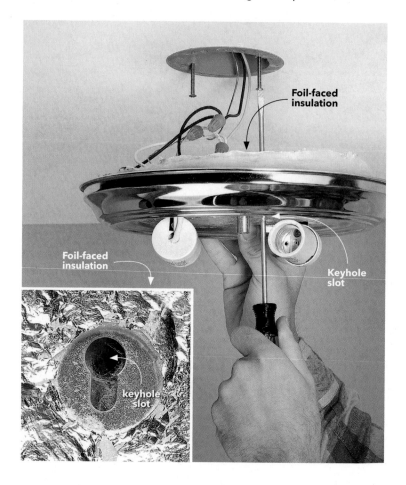

Foil-faced insulation

Foil-faced insulation

Keyhole slot

keyhole slot

Tidy Paint Mixing

Mixing paint is messy, but here's a neat solution. Drill a hole through the paint can or bucket lid, insert a mixer through the hole and then put the lid back on the container. Now you can mix the paint without splashing it everywhere. This also works great for driveway sealant and anything else you have to mix in large quantities

Airtight Paint Cans

If you store paint cans upside down, the paint itself forms an airtight seal around the rim. But make sure the cover is on tight! Hold the can upright and shake it vigorously before you open it so the paint solids drop off the lid.

TABLECLOTH DROP CLOTH

Vinyl tablecloths—the kind usually used on picnic tables—make great drop cloths. They're tougher than plastic sheeting, and if you put the smooth side down, they don't slip around on hard flooring the way canvas drop cloths do. On carpet, put the smooth side up. They're also cheaper than drop cloths—just a few dollars at discount stores.

SPINDLE PAINTER

Use an old sock for a neat, fast way to paint stair spindles or other hard-to-brush objects. First, put on a rubber or latex glove, then slip the sock over your gloved hand. Dip your covered hand into the paint and apply it. You'll cover the entire surface, including all the details.

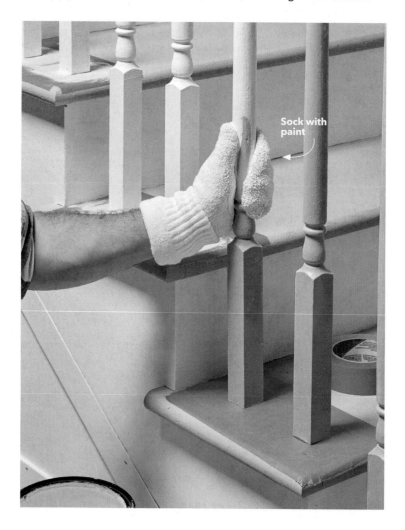

Sock with paint

No More Glue Stains

To prevent stains caused by oozing glue along joints, clamp the pieces together without glue. Put tape on the joint, then cut through it with a sharp blade. Separate the pieces, apply the glue and clamp them together again. The glue will ooze onto the tape, not the wood. Peel off the tape before the glue dries.

Better Paint Stirrer

Instead of using a paint stick to stir your paint, use an old kitchen whisk. It mixes the paint better and it's a lot faster.

PAINT PRESERVERS

Save leftover paint in Mason jars for future touch-ups. A well-sealed jar keeps the paint usable longer than the can does, and it's easier to store. Label the jar with the room the paint was used in.

SAVE THAT CAULK

Don't discard half-used caulk tubes just because the nozzle is plugged with dried caulk. Slit the nozzle on both sides and pry out the plug. Then tape the nozzle halves back together with electrical tape and get back to work.

Removing Paint Drips

Thought you could cut in around wood trim without taping it off, huh? Nice try. Now the paint's dry and you have to remove it. Scraping removes the big blotches but leaves paint in the wood grain. So it's really a two-step process. Start by taping off the wall with painter's tape. Then with light pressure, use a putty knife and scrape off the largest blotches of paint **(top photo)**. Next, scrub off the remaining paint with an old toothbrush soaked in paint remover, working in the direction of the wood grain **(bottom photo)**.

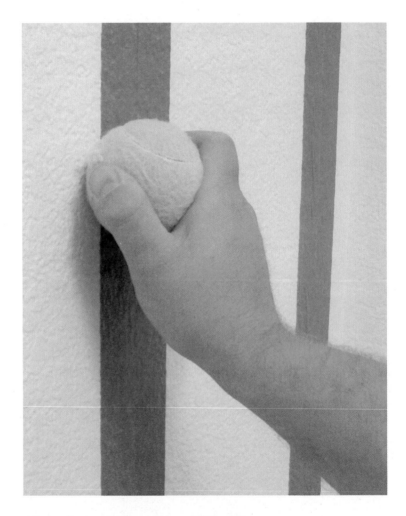

Taping Bumpy Walls

Getting painter's tape to stick well to a semi-smooth wall is a challenge, but here's a great method to make it work. Use a tennis ball to smooth the tape. The ball lets you apply more pressure over a larger area than fingers alone. Grab an older tennis ball which has more give and works better than a brand-new one.

ADD FRACTIONS FAST

Adding 1-13/16 in. to 3-3/8 in. (or any fractions) doesn't have to hurt. Just line up two rulers or tape measures side by side and read the answer instantly, with complete accuracy. It works for subtraction, too—just read the numbers in the other direction.

Final measurement

Line up ruler at first measurement

SAVE THOSE CAPS!

Instead of tossing your old aerosol can caps, save them to use as mixing containers for epoxy. You can usually reuse the caps a couple of times because the leftover hardened epoxy peels away from the slick surface.

Concrete Slide

Pouring a concrete pad is quite a job. But with this clever tip you can do it with ease—instead of schlepping concrete from the mixer to the hole, one wheelbarrow at a time. Use a plastic slide from an old swing set as a chute. Then simply pour the concrete directly into the form.

Wire Soldering Made Easier

It can be tricky to hold wires together to solder them, even when using alligator clips to clasp things in place. Try adding a simple washer to hold everything in place. Clamp the wires on each side of the washer with alligator clips. The hole in the washer gives you nearly 360-degree access to the solder joint.

Dish Soap Wire Lubricant

Whenever pulling wire through a long run of metal or PVC conduit, first squirt some liquid dish soap into the conduit at the feed point of the pull. Then, as you feed the wire and your helper pulls, continue to add a squirt of soap every 10 ft. or so. The soap acts as a lubricant, and the wire glides through with minimal resistance. You can buy special wire lubricant, but dish soap is much cheaper and as close as the kitchen. Plus, this is probably the only remodeling job that leaves your hands cleaner than when you started!

EASY ANGLE CUTS

Here's a quick and reliable way to cut 45-degree angles on a band saw. Just use the lip on a speed square as a guide against your saw table's edge. No setting up a miter gauge!

Speed square

SIMPLE JIGSAW GUIDE

Here's a simple way to make exact cuts with your jigsaw, especially if the lighting or sawdust makes the blade hard to see. Put a piece of tape on the front edge of the saw boot and mark a line following with the path of the saw blade. Now you can easily follow the layout and cut clean, accurate lines.

Nonstick Clamping

When you're making a panel by gluing together several boards, clamp cauls near the ends of the boards to keep them aligned as the glue sets. To keep the cauls from sticking to the panel, enclose them in plastic wrap. When you remove the clamps, just scrape the wrap free from the hardened glue.

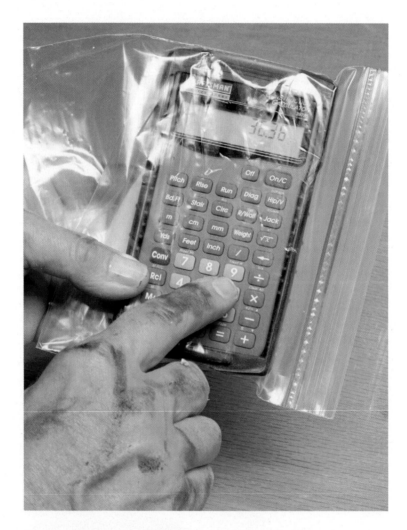

Dust-Free Shop Calculator

Have you had to throw out a calculator (or two!) because the keys
started sticking from all the gunk built up on the keyboard while it
was in the shop? To protect it moving forward, keep it in a plastic bag.
When the bag gets grimy, just toss it instead of the calculator.

UTILITY KNIFE BLADE I.D.

It's not always easy to tell which side of your utility knife blade has already been used. Skip the guesswork with this simple tip. Before you refill the spare blades in your utility knife, mark the sides of each blade with a "1" and a "2." When it's time to replace the blade, use the No. 1 side first. When that side becomes dull, flip it to the No. 2 side. When that gets dull, toss out the blade and start over.

PVC PIPE BLADE AND BIT ORGANIZER

Who doesn't seem to always have extra bits, jigsaw blades and other small items lying loose in their toolboxes and bags? To keep things organized, cut different diameters of PVC pipe to the lengths needed for the accessories. Glue one end cap in place, put the items inside and slide on the other end cap. Use a marker to label each container and you'll be able to find all your bits, blades, screws, etc., when you need them.

MARK YOUR BRADS

When you're in the shop, rip off the tops of all your boxes of brads and mark the sizes on the little tabs **(photo top)**. No more guessing or digging around for the correct length. And when you're working away from the shop and have just a little bit of trim work to pin up that requires more than one size brad, use this tip. Preload the magazine of your gun with an inch or two of the sizes you'll need **(photo bottom)**. Swap them around as you need them. No more hauling around boxes of brads or dealing with broken, hard-to-pack strips.

Ladder Padding

If you spend a lot of time on a ladder, you know that leaning against the rungs all day can take a toll on your shins and thighs. Use this smart tip and slit pieces of kids' swim noodles lengthwise and wrap them around the front of the rungs. Instant relief! The cushions are easy to move as you work. Just make sure you never stand on them. Always place them higher than you'll step since they can create an unsteady surface or fall off if you stand on them.

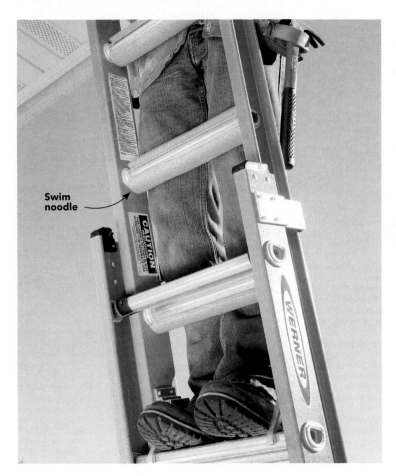

Swim noodle

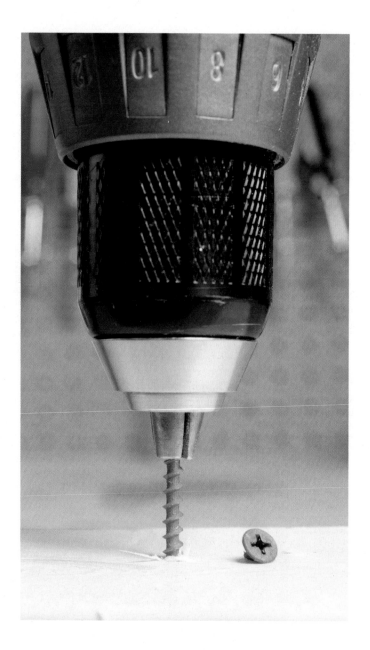

Easy Wood Screw Removal

When you're driving a screw into a board and the head breaks off, try this timesaving trick. Don't hunt around for your locking pliers to pull it out. Instead, use the tool that's already in your hand—your drill. Just loosen the chuck and tighten it around the screw shank. Then reverse the drill and out comes the broken screw. Toss the screw and keep on trucking.

NO SQUARE? NO PROBLEM!

Here's a cool trick for marking a square line across a board with nothing but a handsaw and a pencil. Place the saw (teeth up) on the board and rotate it until the reflection in the saw lines up with the edges of the board itself, then draw your line.

Board reflection

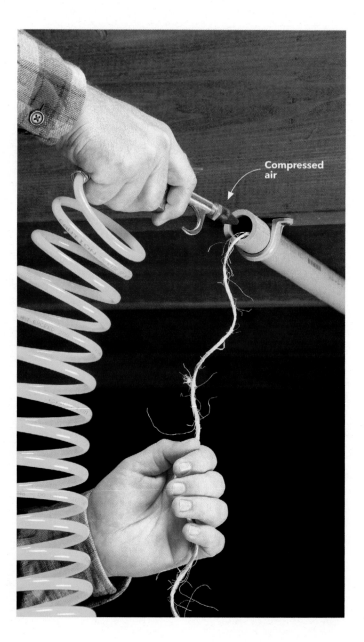

Compressed air

MAKE FISHING WIRES A "BREEZE"

When you run electrical wiring through the conduit mounted underneath your deck or rafters, it can be tricky to get the wire to it's destination. Here's a brilliant solution: Use an air compressor to blow twine through the conduit. It works like a dream! Tie the wiring to a piece of twine slightly longer than the conduit. Use the compressor to blow the twine to the opposite end and then pull it and the wiring through.

Clog-Free Belt Sanding

When you clean new treated deck boards with a belt sander to prep the wood for a semitransparent stain, the gunk from the boards can clog the belt. To keep the belt clean and make it last longer, screw a wire brush to the sawhorse and every so often touch the running belt to the brush. It cleans the belt up nicely—and your deck will look great.

Keep Glue Fresh

Tired of having your glue harden before you get a chance to use it all? Store it upside down. Glue, especially polyurethane glue, hardens when exposed to air. But when the bottle is upside down, no air can get in, so the glue stays fresh.

To build a glue bottle rack, drill a hole the size of the spout into a piece of wood, make sure the cap is on tight, then set the glue bottle in. Leave some wood on the bottom of the hole, so any drips will be confined to the rack and not run all over your workbench. But here's the best part: The glue will be ready to squeeze out when you need it—no more shaking glue down from the bottom!

CABINET HANDLE JIG

When remodeling your kitchen with new door fronts on the cabinets, you'll want to make sure each new cabinet door handle is in the right spot. To do this, make a jig from a 4 x 7-in. plywood scrap and nail a piece of 1x2 over two edges of the plywood. Then mark and drill the screw locations on the jig. This works great for both two-hole and one-hole handles. Because the jig's lip overhangs both faces, it works for right- or left-hinged doors.

Jig

Door handle

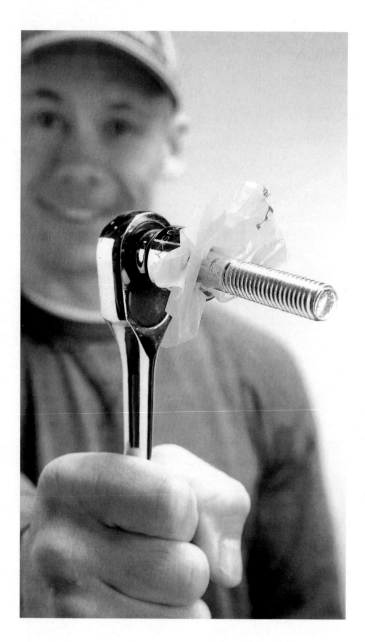

SOCKET WRENCH HELPER

When you're using a socket wrench to ratchet on a bolt in a spot where your fingers can't reach, how do you keep the bolt from falling out of the socket? Simple. Stick a little piece of plastic bag between the bolt head and the socket. The plastic holds the bolt tight while you get it into place, then falls right off when you take the socket off the bolt.

Simple Outfeed Support

Ripping the last few feet of a long board without a helper or support at the other end is virtually impossible. You can solve the problem with an expensive roller support. If you don't have one, set up a temporary outfeed support with clamps, two 2x4s and plywood.

To make a temporary outfeed table, clamp two 8-ft. 2x4s to the saw table, cantilevering them about 5 ft. over the outfeed side. Then screw or clamp 1/4-in. plywood to the underside of the 2x4s. Clamped to the saw table, the 2x4s keep the plywood perfectly flush with the table surface. The boards you're cutting slide onto the support without getting stuck.

This works only for contractor-size and larger table saws with heavy tables. It could cause lighter bench-top saws to tip or bend. If your saw is too light, add 2x4 support legs to the end of the plywood.

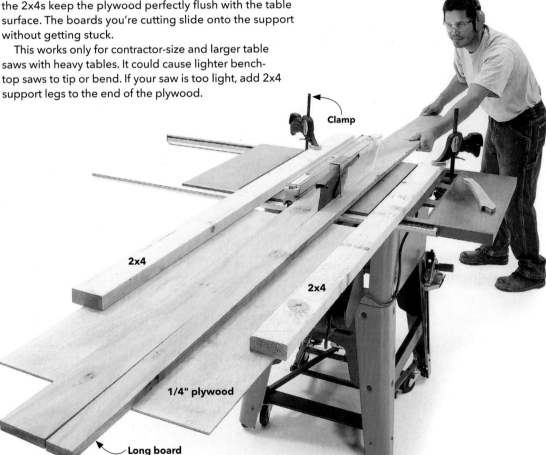

Clamp

2x4

2x4

1/4" plywood

Long board

Quick-Draw Measuring Tape

The clip on a measuring tape can fray the pockets of your jeans. To prevent damage, unscrew the clip and screw a pot magnet in its place. Then hook the clip onto your pocket. It's easy to grab the tape and put it back when done.

Magnet

Tape
measure clip

5-GALLON BUCKET
PVC PIPE CUTTER

Here's a nifty way to cut PVC pipe on the fly. Just make a couple of notches in the top of a 5-gallon bucket. Set the pipe in the notches and you've got a stable spot for sawing. As a bonus, you can load up the bucket and carry your tools along, too.

TAPE TRICKS

Tips to get the most from duct, masking, silicone tapes and more

TAPE REMOVAL TRICK

If you've ever used double-sided tape on a woodworking project, you know how tough it is to get under the tape edge to pull it away from your project when you're done. Here's a trick: Make a tape "handle" by letting the tape hang over the edge of the project a little bit. When it's time to remove the tape, just tug on the handle and it comes off easily.

Soften Old Masking Tape

Who hasn't grabbed an old roll of masking tape and spent the next 15 minutes trying to peel off even an inch or two before it tore jaggedly on the roll? To end this frustration, put the roll in the microwave for about 10 seconds. It softens the adhesive just enough to peel the tape easily off the roll.

Add Silicone Tape to Your Fix-It Kit

Silicone tape is different from other kinds of tape because it's self-fusing—it sticks to itself, not the surface it's being applied to. So it doesn't matter if a drainpipe you're taping is wet or greasy. Another advantage of this tape is that when it's removed, there's no sticky residue. One manufacturer claims the tape will withstand heat up to 500 degrees F and remain flexible down to minus 85 degrees F.

Besides being a temporary solution to a leaky trap, the tape can be used for a litany of projects: weatherproofing, sealing leaking drain lines, wrapping sport and tool grip handles, harnessing cables, keeping rope ends from fraying, hose repair, corrosion protection and more. It really is a versatile product.

The tape is relatively expensive (a 12-ft. roll costs about $6) and may not completely replace your duct or electrical tape, but it's worth adding to your workshop arsenal. Having a roll in your glove box may not be a bad idea either. Rescue Tape, F4 Tape and Tommy Tape are a few name brands. If your local hardware store doesn't stock silicone tape, find it online.

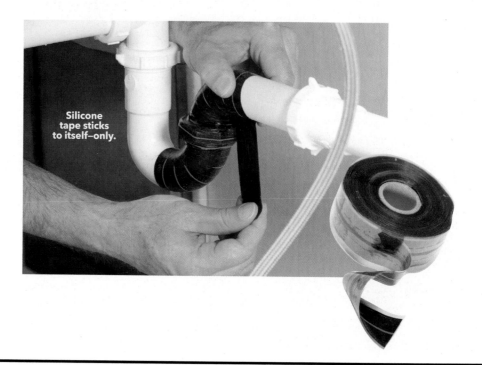

Silicone tape sticks to itself—only.

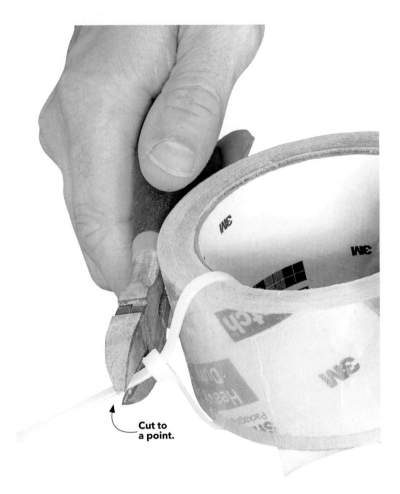

**Cut to
a point.**

HOMEMADE TAPE DISPENSER

No packing tape dispenser? No worries. Use this clever technique to
pack and tape the boxes quickly. Wrap a heavy-duty zip tie around the
roll of tape and trim the tie to a point. After applying a length of tape
to a box, poke the cut end of the zip tie into the tape, it will tear easily.

BEYOND BASIC DUCT TAPE

Duct tape isn't just duct tape anymore. As with coffee, there's an expanding—and confusing—variety of tapes available. Home centers that used to carry one or two types now carry five or six. Online suppliers carry even more, including all the tapes shown below. Here are the subspecies of duct tape that we think are the most useful.

CLASSIC

This is the standard stuff you need for standard jobs. It's priced at $6 or less, so you can afford to keep rolls in strategic locations—toolbox, shop, cars—and be ready for anything. But, despite its name, don't use it—or any type of "duct" tape—on ducts. Metal foil tape is a far better choice for ductwork.

TRANSPARENT

A duct-tape repair can be effective but ugly. Though transparent tape isn't invisible, it blends in for a better-looking fix. The version shown here, Tesa 4665, is also UV-resistant, so it doesn't crumble in sunlight. Duck Tape Clear and Scotch Tough Transparent are other examples. Prices start at about $7.

HEAVY-DUTY

Duct tapes are not created equal. Some have thicker, stronger adhesive and tougher backing. One way to identify these premium tapes is the size of the roll: You'll get a similar length of tape, but the roll will be fatter because of the thicker material. Price is a good guide too; heavy-duty tapes cost about twice as much as standard duct tape. Gorilla Tape (shown here), Intertape Armour Tough and Scotch Tough Extreme Hold ($10) are a few examples.

REMOVABLE

Super-sticky adhesive is what makes duct tape so handy. But it also leaves a gooey mess when you pull up the tape. That's why clever chemists have come up with removable formulas. For about $9, you get the holding power without the residue. Duck Removable (shown here) and Scotch Tough No Residue are two options.

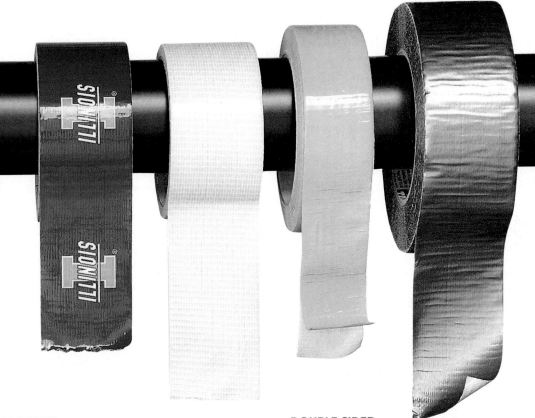

DESIGNER

Just because duct tape is practical doesn't mean it has to be plain. You'll find quite a few patterns and colors on store shelves, especially at craft stores. For a fun selection of colors, patterns and more, go to walmart.com. College logo tapes cost about $7.

GLOW-IN THE-DARK

Can't find your flashlight in the dark? Make it glow with duct tape. IPG's FireFly tape works just like other glow-in-the-dark items; it gives off a greenish glow after being exposed to light. It comes in plain off-white or a zebra pattern for about $9.

DOUBLE-SIDED

Unlike most double-sided tapes, this is true duct tape, complete with the strong adhesive and tough mesh. Like others, it has a peel-off backing. Don't remove the backing until it's stuck in place—it will stick to your finger and itself and you'll end up with a wad of useless tape. Duck Double-Sided and Shurtape Double-Sided are two examples (about $9).

OUTDOOR

If you've used duct tape outside, you know that after a few months in the sun, the backing turns flaky and falls off, leaving a gritty residue. No duct tape is completely immune to UV sunlight, but Scotch Tough Heavy Duty All-Weather ($9) will last about three times as long, according to the manufacturer.

REBUILD YOUR RATCHET

An inexpensive kit can rescue this handy tool

GOT A RATCHET THAT'S JAMMED, RUSTED OR WON'T SWITCH DIRECTIONS? Don't toss it, rebuild it. In most cases, you can get yours back into shape with just a good cleaning and new grease. But if you've broken a spring or a pawl, you'll need to buy a rebuilding kit. To find one for yours, just enter the ratchet brand and model number in a search engine, or try ebay.com.

Before you buy a kit, disassemble the ratchet to assess its condition. Use a combination snap ring pliers (one option is Tekton No. 3578) to remove the internal or external snap ring from the ratchet head **(Photo 1).** Or use a small flat-blade screwdriver to remove a spiral snap ring **(Photo 2)**. If your ratchet

doesn't use snap rings, it'll come apart with either a hex wrench or a screwdriver.

Throw a towel over the ratchet (to capture flying springs) and slide the entire ratchet assembly out of the head. Clean the parts with brake cleaner and an old toothbrush. Remove any rust with a rust removal chemical. If the spring ends are intact and the pawl teeth are sharp, you can reuse them. If not, buy a rebuild kit. Then apply a light coating of wheel bearing grease to all the parts. Don't use engine oil; it'll just drip out. And don't pack the head with grease—that'll prevent the pawl from reversing. Then reassemble **(Photo 3)**.

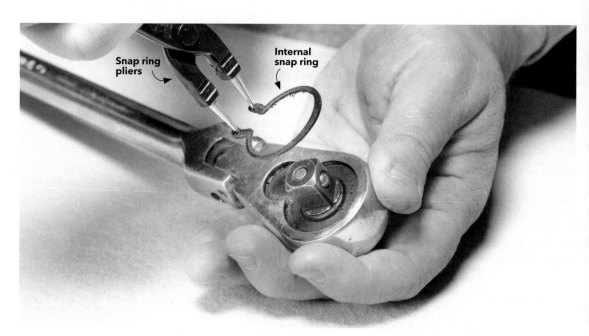

Snap ring pliers

Internal snap ring

1 **Remove an internal/external snap ring.** Insert the prongs of the snap ring pliers into the holes on the snap ring. Then compress the internal snap ring and lift it out of the retaining slot. Change the pliers over to external mode to expand an external snap ring.

Spiral snap ring

2 **Remove a spiral snap ring.** Locate the clipped end of the spiral snap ring and twist it out and up with a small flat-blade screwdriver. Then "unwind" the snap ring in a counterclockwise direction. Reverse the procedure to reinstall.

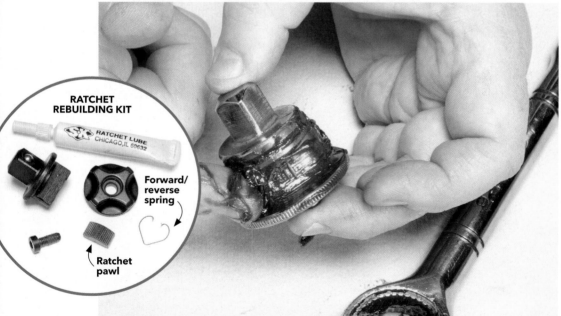

RATCHET REBUILDING KIT

RATCHET LUBE
CHICAGO,IL 60632

Forward/ reverse spring

Ratchet pawl

3 **Grease and reassemble.** Compress the pawl assembly with your fingers and slide the entire ratchet into the head. Rotate it in both directions to check the pawl's operation and spread the grease. Then reinstall the snap ring or screws. Double-check the operation.

CHAPTER 5

EASY FIXES

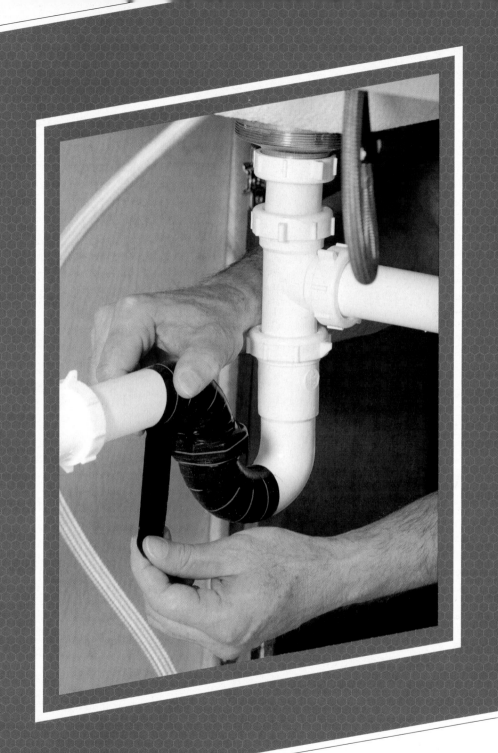

DUST CATCHER

Drilling holes in drywall is messy. The dust floats all over and is a pain to clean up. To contain the dust when you're drilling into a ceiling, poke the shaft of the drill bit through a box before chucking it into your drill

GOLF TEE TO THE RESCUE

This tip you'll use often, especially to repair stripped-out latch and hinge holes on doors. Often the only problem with a sagging door or a door that won't latch is a loose hinge or strike plate. And the looseness is usually the result of a stripped screw hole.

The solution is to apply a dab of one-hour epoxy to a golf tee, then tap the tee into the screw hole. After an hour, chisel off the excess and you'll have solid wood that will hold new screws. For tiny holes, use a few toothpicks instead of a tee.

Hassle-Free Picture Hanging

When you're hanging a picture that has a wire across the back, it's hard to get your hand behind the picture to guide the wire over the hook Try this: Slide a piece of string between the hook and the wall. Holding both ends of the string, pull it under the wire and lower the picture into place. The string guides the wire right over the hook. Drop one end of the string and release it from the hook. Done.

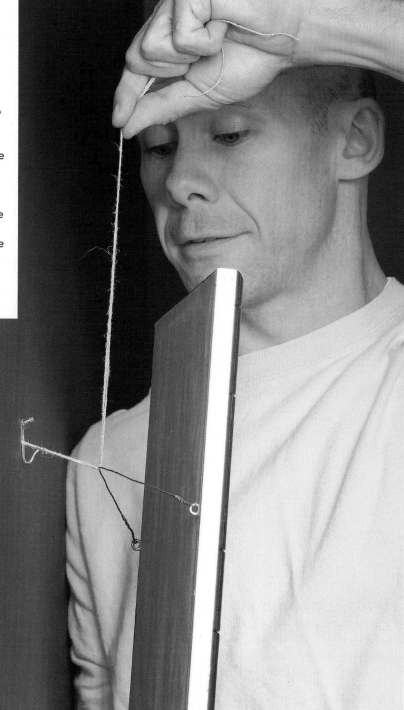

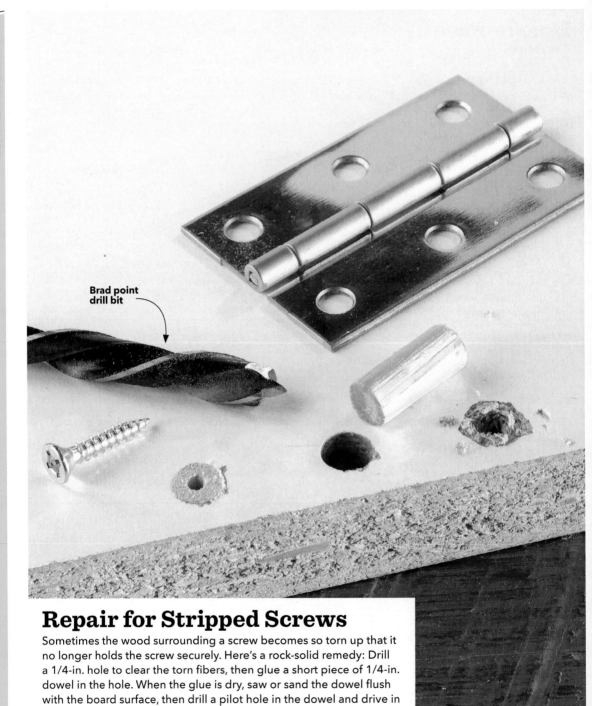

Brad point
drill bit

Repair for Stripped Screws

Sometimes the wood surrounding a screw becomes so torn up that it no longer holds the screw securely. Here's a rock-solid remedy: Drill a 1/4-in. hole to clear the torn fibers, then glue a short piece of 1/4-in. dowel in the hole. When the glue is dry, saw or sand the dowel flush with the board surface, then drill a pilot hole in the dowel and drive in the screw.

EASY-CLIP TREE ORNAMENTS

The wire hooks that come with Christmas tree ornaments can be hard to use and can scratch the ornaments. Instead of wire hangers, use plastic-coated paper clips to hang ornaments. They're stronger and easy to use, and best of all, they won't scratch the ornaments, so you can leave them attached when you pack the ornaments away at the end of each season.

Plastic-coated paper clip

STAY-PUT DOOR HOLDER

Do you have problems keeping your door from blowing shut in the summer? Put a piece of adhesive-backed Velcro fastener on the doorstop and another piece on the wall. The door will stay open until you pull it free.

Loose Nail Solution

Here's a trick to hang a picture using an existing nail hole when the hole is a little too big and the nail slides in too far. Rather than making a new nail hole, put a tiny dab of super glue on the tip of the nail, push it into the hole and hold it in place. After 30 seconds, the nail will be tight and you can hang the picture.

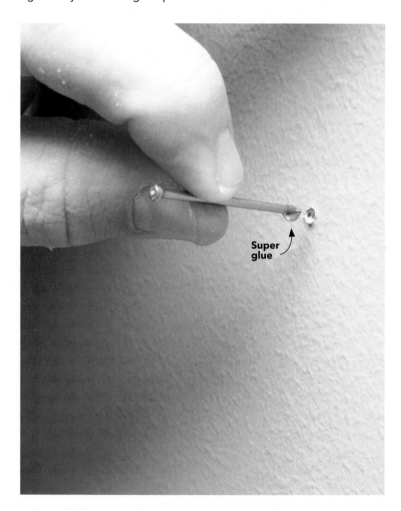

Super glue

Keyway

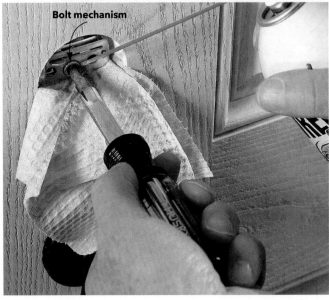

Bolt mechanism

Free Up a Sticking Dead Bolt

Dead bolt jammed? Don't panic; it's just crying for a few shots of lube. Dry Teflon lube spray is your best bet. Start by lubing the lock cylinder (**photo top**). Leave the lock cylinder on the door and spray inside the keyway. Then insert your key and twist it several times to work in the lube. If that doesn't free it, you'll need to lube the bolt mechanism (**photo bottom**). Remove the two screws that hold the lock cylinder and pull it from the door. Then saturate the bolt mechanism with the spray lube and twist it back and forth with a flat-blade screwdriver. Reinstall the lock cylinder and you are good to go.

FROZEN LOCK TRICK

If you're struggling to open a frozen lock, squirt hand sanitizer on your key and then put it in the lock. This might take a minute, but it should defrost the lock so you can turn it. (And who doesn't have hand sanitizer handy?

Hand sanitizer

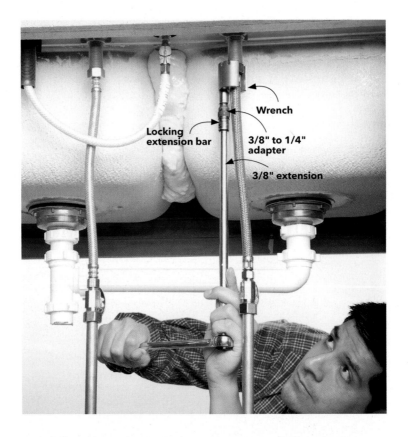

Wrench

Locking
extension bar

3/8" to 1/4"
adapter

3/8" extension

COOL FAUCET-REMOVAL WRENCH

Replacing a faucet is easy once you get the retaining nuts off. But
that's easier said than done. If you're like most DIY plumbers, you
probably use a cheap basin wrench. That means shimmying under
the sink, which is tricky.

Forget that. Just buy a Basin Buddy wrench and snap it onto a long,
3/8-in. extension from your socket set. To use, slide the open end
of the wrench over the supply tube and push it up to the faucet nuts.
Then turn the ratchet and it will self-center on the nut. Remove and
reattach the ratchet handle as you rotate the nut. You'll save your back
and do the job in a fraction of the time.

Bucket Bungee

If you use a lot of 5-gallon pails to store tools and other construction gear in your pickup, but find it frustrating that they are always sliding around and tipping over, worry no more. Here's a great solution: Secure them in the pickup bed with bungee cords. Now they will stay put!

Bungee cord

Picture Frame Bumpers

After painting interior walls, protect them from marks from pictures with rubber bumpers attached to the bottom corners of frames. The rubber holds the pictures level and protects the fresh wall paint.

Crawl Space Helper

The crawl space under many houses may be a bit tight. So when you need to go "down under," you'll want to have all the needed supplies with you the first time down, to prevent multiple trips. Load everything up in a concrete mixing pan and drag it along as you move around down there. An old plastic snow sled would work great too.

A BETTER STRAW FOR EXPANDING FOAM

Expanding foam is so useful with its many advantages, but it can be messy and hard to control. And since you need to hold the can upside down, it's nearly impossible to get it into tight areas such as pipe penetrations in rim joists. Here's a great way to get into those difficult spots. Replace the short straw with a length of 1/8-in. vinyl tubing. Not only is it way easier to control, but you can hold the can upside down and deliver the foam wherever you need it.

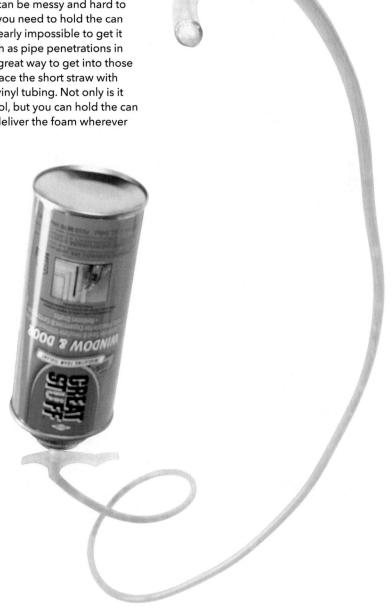

HIDE A HOLE WITH SMOKE DETECTOR

Here's an inexpensive but useful way to fix a large hole in your ceiling. Install a smoke detector over it! Not only will you not have to patch, sand, and paint the area, you'll also be adding a safety devise to your home.

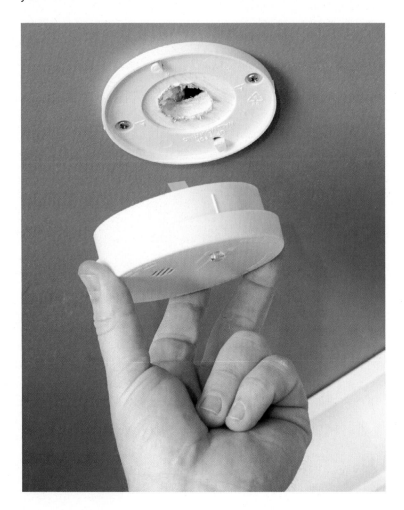

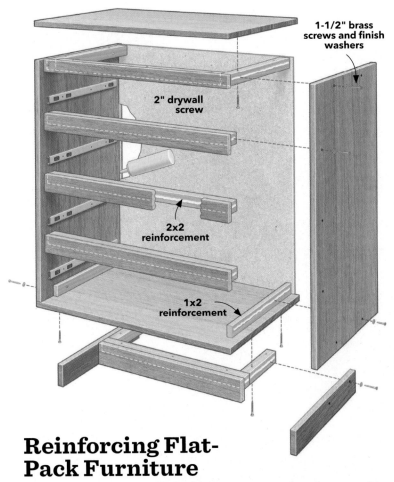

1-1/2" brass screws and finish washers

2" drywall screw

2x2 reinforcement

1x2 reinforcement

Reinforcing Flat-Pack Furniture

Flat-pack furniture, those that come in a flat box and require assembly, can be useful. Some brands are better than others, but cheaper versions can get wobbly or fall apart over time. That doesn't always mean the furniture is a total loss. With some 2x2s and 1x2s, screws and a bit of glue, you can reinforce and save the piece to live another day. It's the connections that generally fail, because the particleboard just isn't as strong as real wood. Use any or all of the placements shown to strengthen the connections and help your furniture last.

Don't Stock Up on Spray Foam

Every spring and fall, home centers offer great prices on insulating spray foam. If you're tempted to stock up, be prepared to use it right away. Most people don't know that the cans have a one-year shelf life—and that's one year from the date of manufacture, not the date of purchase. Some manufacturers print an expiration date on the bottom of the can as shown. But others use a cryptic production code. If you buy that product, make sure you use it as soon as possible.

BEST IF USED BY:
15:36 18/JAN/2012

LB fitting

HIDE A HOUSE KEY IN PLAIN SIGHT

Burglars can easily find a house key hidden under a mat or over the door molding, but they'll never think to look inside plastic conduit. Just glue 1/2-in. plastic conduit to a 1/2-in. LB fitting. Drive the conduit into the ground next to the house so it looks as if the conduit enters there. You can leave out the bottom screw or just glue a screw in place to completely fool the crooks. Leave the top screw a little loose so the cover will swivel open easily. Pop the key inside and no one's the wiser (except you—and all the thieves reading this tip!).

LIGHT SHROUD MADE OF PVC

Going crazy from your neighbor's new septic system with the brilliant red light on the top that lets them know the unit is working but is so bright that it's like having a harbor navigation buoy in the yard?! Get permission to build a shroud from 3-in. plastic pipe. Then cut out a little slot in the shroud, slip on a cap and caulk it down over the light. Now your neighbors can see the beacon from their kitchen window, but the light won't keep you up all night!

Wine Cork Garden Markers

Save your wine corks (and collect them from friends) to use as garden markers. Label the cork with a permanent marker, then stick a skewer into the cork and poke the skewer into the ground at the end of the corresponding row.

"Hot" Hose Tip

If you're trying to repair a hose by installing a new fitting, you may find it pretty tough to wrestle the barbed end into a stiff rubber hose. Make it easier by softening the end of the hose in a bucket or teakettle of hot water.

HIGH-VISIBILITY TOOLS

Ever have trouble keeping track of gardening tools while working in the yard because they seem to disappear into the grass? Wrap the handles with fluorescent tape so they're easier to spot.

Duct tape

BETTER TREE WATERING

Tired of hauling buckets of water to distant trees and dumping the water at the base of the tree only to see it quickly run off? Take some old 5-gallon buckets and drill a 1/4-in. hole near the bottom of each one. After plugging the holes with dowels, fill the buckets and haul them to the trees (a wheelbarrow will help). Then unplug the holes; it will take several minutes for the buckets to drain, allowing the soil to soak up every drop.

Filler for Big Planters

Add empty cans and broken clay pots to a deep planter to cut down on the amount of soil you'll need to fill it. The cans and pots also improve drainage and aeration.

Large-Print Lawn Guide

When it's time to apply herbicides and fertilizers, how much time do you waste looking for your glasses because you can't read the tiny print that shows the correct application rates? Be annoyed no more. Instead write the information in large print on the spreader and hose end sprayer. Now when you are ready to use the spreader, no need to search for gllasses!

WEATHER-PROOF PLANT LABELS

Labeling your garden is valuable especially in large gardens. But so many label methods can't stand up to constant sun and moisture. Here are two solutions that stand up to any kind of weather.

Start with a label maker and some recycled vinyl window blinds. Cut the slats into 9-in. lengths and stick on the labels (**photo top**).

Or, slip a small zip-top plastic bag over the seed packet, with the bag upside-down so the rain doesn't get in (**photo bottom**). Place the packet over a stake and seal the zipper as far as possible.

2" PVC

FERTILIZING DENSE PLANTS

To get fertilizer to the base of bushes and other dense plants, use a length of 2-in. PVC. Slide one end down to the plant base and pour the fertilizer into the pipe. Cut the top of the pipe at 45 degrees to give yourself a larger opening for pouring.

Handy Branch Hauler

Need a way to haul branches over to your fire pit? Carrying them in your arms is dirty work, and trying to stuff them into a plastic bag is awkward. Try using a sturdy shopping bag with handles. Slit the sides, lay it flat and fill it with branches and small logs. It loads easily and lets you carry wood without getting your clothes full of sap or mud.

Plastic shopping bag

Simple Veggie Washer

As much as you love growing fresh vegetables in your garden, no one likes all the dirt that comes inside after picking. Here's a great veggie washer. Drill holes in the bottom and sides of a 5-gallon bucket with a 5/8-in. spade bit. Place your fresh-picked veggies in the bucket and hose them off before you bring them inside. The dirt and sand stay out in the garden, and only the veggies end up in your kitchen!

5/8" holes

EASIER MULCH UNLOADING

Buying mulch in bulk at the nursery is economical, but often it gets dumped into the bed of your pickup truck with a front-end loader. Instead of shoveling the mulch onto your driveway to later haul it to where it's needed, here's a much easier method. Load your pickup bed with 5-gallon plastic buckets and have the mulch dumped into the truck as usual. Then use a rake to even out the load so every container is filled up. When it's time to unload, do it one bucket at a time and dump the mulch exactly where you want it. The buckets store nicely in the garage to reuse them throughout the year.

Spreading
shield

EASY-TO-INSTALL PLANT PROTECTOR

Here's a great way to protect your flowers, bushes and grass when you're using a broadcast spreader for weed-and-feed fertilizer or a sand-and-salt mixture for an icy sidewalk. Hang this simple plywood shield on the side of your spreader with a pair of spring clamps.

No More Smelly Lawn Clippings

After mowing, it's common to dump all the lawn clippings into a "green refuse" bin. But after a day or so, the grass clippings turn into a slimy, smelly mess. To combat the stench, throw a few handfuls of shredded paper into the bottom of the barrel. The paper helps absorb the moisture and reduce the smell.

Shredded Paper

Easy-Read Rain Gauge

Drip food coloring into the bottom of your rain gauge the next time you empty it. The coloring tints the rainwater, making the gauge easier to read. This may stain plastic rain gauges.

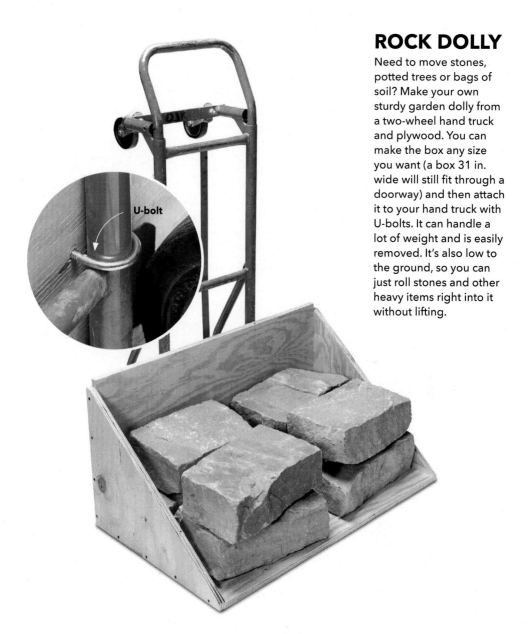

U-bolt

ROCK DOLLY

Need to move stones, potted trees or bags of soil? Make your own sturdy garden dolly from a two-wheel hand truck and plywood. You can make the box any size you want (a box 31 in. wide will still fit through a doorway) and then attach it to your hand truck with U-bolts. It can handle a lot of weight and is easily removed. It's also low to the ground, so you can just roll stones and other heavy items right into it without lifting.

MOWING IN COMFORT

Make mowing a more enjoyable task thanks to pipe insulation taped around the handle. Make sure the insulation doesn't interfere with your auto-shutoff bar, if you have one. No more numb hands and blisters from the bare metal handle!

PUDDLE-FREE LAWN CHAIRS

After a rainstorm, plastic lawn chairs always seem to have a puddle of water in the low spot on the seat and, inevitably, someone sits down on it. Even the newer plastic lawn chairs that come with a predrilled hole in the bottom often collect water. To solve the soggy-bottom problem, pour some water onto the seat to find the puddles and then drill small drain holes in the low spots.

Renew Rubber Gloves

How often do you get holes in the fingertips of your gardening gloves? Here's a way to prolong their life with Flex Seal liquid rubber sealant. After washing the gloves and letting them dry, brush Flex Seal on the fingertips and let them dry overnight. They will last for months if not longer!

Sealant covering a hole

Truck-Bed Liner Extension

When hauling a lot of landscaping materials in your truck, it can be annoying when dirt, leaves and rocks got caught between the tailgate and the bed liner. To remedy this, tuck a piece of thin plywood under the bed to span the gap. You can store it under the mat when it's not in use. Plastic or a thin rubber runner would also work.

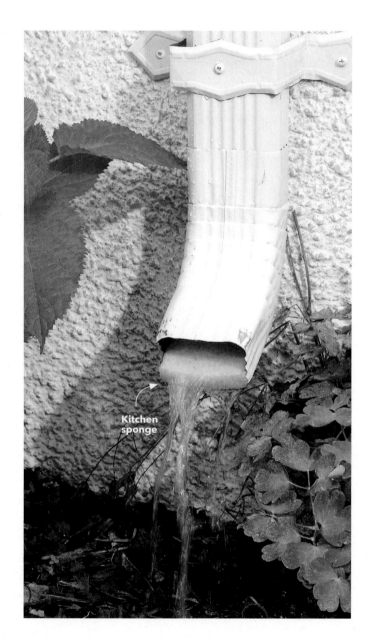

Kitchen sponge

NOISY-DRIP STOPPER

Do you have a noisy drip coming from your downspout that's driving you nuts? Just push a kitchen sponge into the bottom of the downspout. It'll muffle the drip noise without blocking the water flow.

STAND-UP SHOVEL

Do you step out your patio door and into the newly fallen snow? Here's a tip to have a snow shovel always available to for keeping the deck clean quickly. Buy a broom clip at the hardware store and install it on the deck railing. No more digging for the shovel after a storm.

Outsmart Woodpeckers

Keep woodpeckers outside your home by covering all woodpecker holes with metal flashing or tin can lids (fix the actual damage later). Then hang shiny deterrents such as Mylar strips, magnifying mirrors or pinwheels all around the repairs. If that doesn't work, cover the entire side of the house with plastic netting from a garden center, stapling it to secure. Once the woodpeckers leave, you can remove the netting.

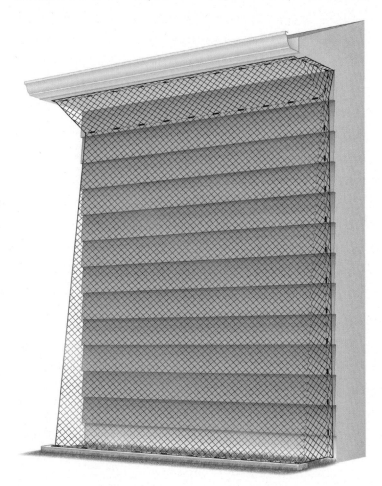

2-HOUR CAMPFIRE BENCH

NEED OUTDOOR SEATING IN A HURRY? This simple bench, based on author and ecologist Aldo Leopold's classic design, can be constructed in a couple of hours. All it takes is two boards and 18 screws, for a cost of less than $25.

Cut the legs from a 2x8 x 10-ft. piece of rot-resistant wood (**photo 1**). Cut the seat and backrest from an 8-ft. 2x8.

Lay out and assemble the sides as mirror images, using the seat and back pieces for alignment (**photo 2**). Join the legs with three 2-1/2-in. deck screws and construction adhesive. Predrill all the screw holes with a countersink bit to avoid splitting the wood. Finally, set the sides up parallel to each other and glue and screw the seat and back into place. Finish the bench with a coat of exterior oil or stain.

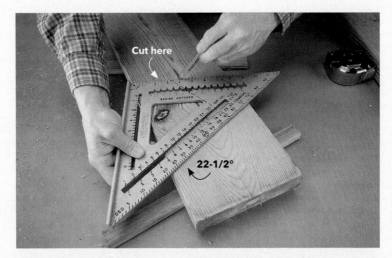

1 Starting at one end of a 10-ft. board, make the same 22-1/2-degree cut five times to create the four legs.

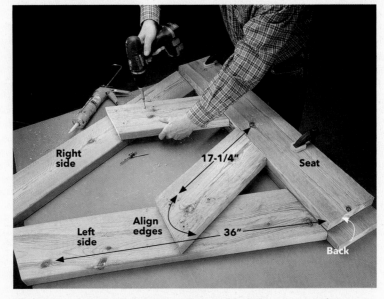

2 Clamp the seat and back to the workbench as a stop, then predrill, glue and screw the rear legs to the front legs.

CUTTING LIST

DIMENSIONS	PART
2x8 x 17-1/4" (22-1/2-degree cuts)	Rear legs
2x8 x 36" (22-1/2-degree cuts)	Front legs
2x8 x 42"	Seat
2x8 x 45"	Back

Note: All cut from 10' 2x8s.

START A GARDEN

Create a planting bed (for flowers or veggies) in 8 easy steps

READY TO START A GARDEN? You could do what one reader did: She threw some topsoil on top of an unused wooden sandbox, let her 6-year-old choose the seeds (strawberries, green beans, watermelon) and watered haphazardly. Net result? They ate a lot of green beans, and most of the rest of the plants were no-shows.

So maybe you would want to start a garden the right way instead—do the planning, test the soil and cultivate the ideal soil conditions for the plants you choose. Here we'll show you how to start a garden—any size!—from scratch. All it takes is basic garden tools. A sod cutter to remove the grass and a rototiller make the job go faster but aren't necessary.

1. TRACK THE SUNLIGHT

The amount of sunlight your garden gets will determine which plants you should choose. You'll have the widest selection of plants to pick from if you place the garden in full sun to light shade. Vegetables require full sun.

You probably have an idea where you want to plant flowers to enhance the landscape. If so, choose plants suited for those growing conditions (such as full sun, partial sun or shade). Take photos of the proposed site throughout the day so that when you shop for flowers, you'll have a reference of how much sun the area gets. If you're flexible on the garden location, choose a spot that suits the sun requirements of the plants you want. Take a trip to a garden center to see what plants are available for your zone and how much sun your favorites will need (visit usna.usda.gov/hardzone/ushzmap.html for a plant hardiness zone map).

Unless you're planning a rain garden, avoid gardening in low spots in the yard where water collects. In the fall, low areas tend to be frost pockets, which can shorten your growing season. A well-drained area will yield the best plants.

2. OUTLINE THE GARDEN BED

Use a garden hose or landscaping paint to mark the perimeter of the garden bed. Avoid creating tight angles that would make it hard to mow around the garden. Gentle curves look more natural than sharp corners. And make the size manageable—you can always add on later if you decide you want a bigger garden.

Don't dig yet. Wait at least one full day so you can look at the site from various vantage points (such as your deck or living room) and at different times of the day. It's a lot easier to change the shape or location now than after you've started digging. Once you decide on the layout, call 811 to have underground utilities marked

2. Mark the garden bed and make sure you're happy with the layout before you start digging.

(for free!). You'll have to identify irrigation lines yourself—they usually run in straight lines between sprinkler heads.

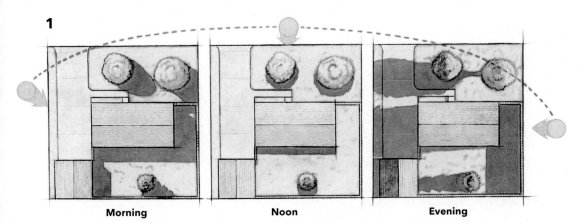

| Morning | Noon | Evening |

1. Take photos of your garden location in the morning, early afternoon and evening to see how much sun it gets. Vegetables and full-sun plants need six hours of daily sun; partial-sun plants require three to six hours; and shade plants need two to three hours.

4. Slice and then dig around the edge of the garden bed to make it easier to follow the shape as you remove or kill the grass. 5. Cut away the sod in the garden with a power sod cutter. Remove the sod and use it in your yard or turn it upside down and start a compost pile.

3. TEST THE SOIL

A soil test will tell you whether you need to add amendments such as lime, nitrogen, phosphorus or potassium to the soil.

Test kits are available at home and garden centers, but use a university extension service or a state-certified soil-testing lab instead to get the most accurate results. Enter "university extension service" and your state in any search engine to find the nearest lab. Contact the lab to get the necessary paperwork to submit with your sample. Dig down 6 in. and scoop up a trowel full of soil. Take samples from 5 to 10 areas in the garden and mix them in a clean bucket. Wait for the soil to dry (this can take several days), then mail it to the extension service. Retest the soil every three to five years.

Send the soil sample, the paperwork and a check to your local extension service. The service will mail back a report telling you the nutrient content of the soil and the type and amount of fertilizer to add. A lab report tells you what nutrients your soil needs.

4. EDGE THE GARDEN

Now that the prep work is done, you can dig and plant your garden in a weekend. The first step is edging the garden bed. Use a square shovel or an edger to dig down about 6 in., slicing through the grass roots around the garden bed. After making the slices, dig around the garden edge at a slight angle to remove a 3-in. swath of grass and create a small trench. This keeps the sod cutter or herbicide from going into your yard when you remove or kill grass in the garden.

5. REMOVE THE SOD

The grass has to go—you can't just till it under or it'll grow back and you'll never get rid of it. Digging up turf is hard work, so do yourself a favor and rent a power sod cutter from a rental center. Set the blade to cut just below the roots and slice the grass into long strips. Then roll the sod into easy-to-carry bundles. Use the sod to fill bare spots in the yard, or compost it to use later in your garden.

6. KEEP OUT GRASS

Add a border to keep grass in your lawn from invading your garden; it's hard to get rid of once it does. Home and garden centers sell a variety of border and edging materials.

Strips of steel, aluminum or heavy-duty plastic (starting at $1.60 per ft.) work best on fairly even terrain and are unobtrusive. Pavers (55¢ apiece and up) form a wide border that allows flowers to spill over and provides a flat surface to mow over. A raised stone wall contains the garden and looks attractive, but at $10 per ft. for a two-course wall, it's the most expensive option. Be sure your border extends at least 4 in. into the ground to keep out grass. Interested in building a low-maintenance border?

Visit familyhandyman.com and search for "borders."

7. FERTILIZE TO SUIT YOUR SOIL

Your soil test will tell you the type of fertilizer your garden needs. Fertilizer labels list the three main nutrients needed for plant growth. A 10-20-10 formula, for example, contains 10 percent nitrogen (N), 20 percent phosphorus (P) and 10 percent potassium (K).

Buy a slow-release granular fertilizer that contains the appropriate percentage of the nutrients your soil needs. If your soil only needs one nutrient, don't bother adding the others (some fertilizers contain just one nutrient, such as a 20-0-0). Apply the fertilizer just before planting.

8. ENRICH THE SOIL

Adding organic matter such as compost, manure or peat moss increases drainage in clay soils and water-holding capacity in sandy soils. It also makes the soil more permeable, which encourages root growth and attracts organisms that leave nutrients in the soil. There isn't one best type of organic matter, so buy whatever's the least expensive in your area.

Spread 2 to 4 in. of organic matter over the garden. You can work it into the top 6 to 10 in. of soil with a shovel by digging down, then flipping the load over to mix the organic matter and soil. But a faster, easier way is to use a rototiller ($45 for four hours at rental centers).

6. Borders provide an attractive finish, stop grass from creeping in and make it easier to mow around the garden. **7.** Spread a slow-release fertilizer on the garden using a handheld spreader for even coverage. **8.** Work organic matter into the soil with a rototiller or a shovel. Organic matter improves drainage and adds nutrients.

GROW A GREAT LAWN

The 6 magic bullets and more!

AS THE IN-HOUSE TURF "EXPERT" at Family Handyman for the past 15 years, I've spent a huge amount of time talking with world-class grass gurus and learning the science of lawns. And I've spent even more time clearing and converting a half-acre of rough, overgrown horse pasture to a Pebble Beach–quality lawn.

My final conclusion is this: Getting great grass is surprisingly simple and easy. If you're willing to learn some basic facts and put in just a few hours of light labor every summer, you can have a lush lawn. The next few pages provide the know-how. You supply the labor.

1. Attack Broadleaf Weeds in Mild Weather

You need to kill weeds when they're growing. That's because the herbicide is absorbed through the leaves and then sent throughout the rest of the plant. When the weather is too cool, the weed isn't growing and the herbicide won't be absorbed, and the chemical isn't as effective. Too hot and the herbicide will stress the grass. The product directions will give you the best temperature range. Apply herbicides when rain isn't forecast; a soaking will just rinse off the herbicide before it can really do any good.

2. Water Deeply, But Not Often

If you water frequently and for short periods, the grass roots have no reason to grow deep. Those shallow roots can't reach deep soil nutrients or deliver the water when you skip a watering. Instead, water deeply enough to penetrate the soil 4 to 6 in. Do our little test (detailed below) for a few waterings and you'll get a sense of just how long and often. It'll depend entirely on weather conditions and your soil type.

Heavy soils should be watered less often and less heavily but for longer periods of time. Sandy soils, on the other hand, can handle heavy, fast watering but dry out faster. In hot, dry weather, you may have to water every two to three days.

Water for 30 minutes. Then plunge a spade into the soil and pry out a wedge to see how far the water has penetrated. Four to 6 in. deep is ideal. Not deep enough? Water longer. Once you know how long to water, use a water timer and you'll know what to set it for every time.

5 Ways to Make It All Easier, Simpler and Cheaper

1. USE A BROADCAST SPREADER—NOT A DROP SPREADER.

Drop spreaders are notoriously tricky to use. You're bound to end up with stripes or checkerboard patterns on your grass. You're much better off with a broadcast spreader, which spews out the granules at random for much more consistent coverage.

2. DON'T TREAT YOUR WHOLE LAWN FOR JUST A FEW WEEDS.

If you have only a few weeds, pull them by hand or spray each one with a pump sprayer.

3. USE A HOSE-END SPRAYER TO KILL A YARD FULL OF WEEDS.

It's faster and more effective to dispense concentrated liquid broadleaf killers than to use granular broadleaf killers. You just add the herbicide, dial in the right concentration on the sprayer lid and walk around the yard and mist all the weeds. You can treat an average yard in less than 20 minutes.

4. RESEED IN THE LATE SUMMER OR EARLY FALL.

Whether you're seeding a small patch or a whole yard, you're going to be much more successful if you wait for the cooler, damper weather of early spring, late summer or early fall. It's almost impossible to get seed to survive during the dog days of summer. It's simply too hot and dry.

5. USE CONCENTRATES WHENEVER YOU CAN.

For most liquids, you can buy concentrates and mix your own treatment with water. You'll save about 70 percent of the cost of premixed. Mix only as much as you can use within a week or two. Minerals in tap water will reduce the potency.

3. Kill Crabgrass Before It Sprouts

Crabgrass preventers (aka preemergence treatments) do one thing and one thing only. They prevent crabgrass (and any other seed) from sprouting. Once crabgrass sprouts, it's too late.

Here's the key: Apply preventer between the second and the third mowings. Because crabgrass starts sprouting a few weeks after the grass greens up, that's generally just the right time.

4. Don't Skip Fall Fertilizing

Before the lawn goes to sleep for the winter, you should feed it well. Even after the grass seems to go dormant, the roots are soaking up nutrients and storing energy for the next growing season. Surprisingly, it's much more important to fertilize in the fall than in the spring, when most people do it. Like watering, this is one of the most important favors you can do for your lawn.

5. Don't Cut the Grass Too Short

Every grass type has an optimal cutting height. And you're better off on the high side of that height. Here are a few reasons: The grass blade is the food factory of the plant. Short blades just can't generate as much food as long blades. Long blades also shade and cool the soil. That means weed seeds are less likely to sprout, and you won't have to water as often because water won't evaporate as fast.

Not sure what type of grass you have? Take a sample to a garden center for help. Or go to scotts.com and click on "grass type identifier" at the bottom of the page. Compare your sample with the ones shown.

6. Test the Soil pH Level

Grass grows best when it's growing in the "pH happy zone." If the soil is too acidic or too alkaline, the grass won't thrive even if you do everything else right. So collect one tablespoon-size sample a couple of inches under the sod in three different places in your yard and take the three samples in for testing. Some garden centers offer the service, or search the internet for "soil testing" to find a place to send it.

You're after a pH between 6 and 7.2. If it's too high, you'll treat the lawn with iron sulfate or sulphur; too low and you'll use pelletized limestone. Whoever does the testing will tell you what and how much to use to fix the pH. Applying the treatment is as easy as walking around the yard with a spreader.

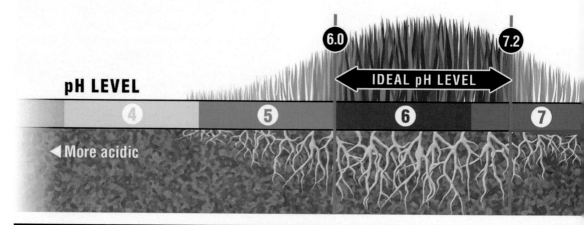

12 Pearls of Lawn Wisdom

1. DON'T MOW WET GRASS.
You'll leave giant clumps of sodden clippings where they'll smother the grass beneath. Not only that, it'll carpet the underside of your mower deck with a thick mat.

2. SET YOUR SPREADER AT HALF THE RECOMMENDED DOSAGE AND TREAT THE LAWN TWICE FROM OPPOSITE DIRECTIONS.
It'll take twice as much hoof work on your part, but you'll get a more consistent distribution.

3. FILL THE SPREADER ON THE DRIVEWAY, NOT OVER THE GRASS.
Or at least spread a tarp on the grass to catch spillage. If you have an accident, you'll have a nice, big dead spot in your lawn.

4. ACCEPT THAT YOU CAN'T GROW GRASS EVERYWHERE.
If you've struggled mightily to grow grass in a shady spot, at some point give it up and mulch, use a shade-tolerant ground cover or plan yourself a patio.

5. GIVE CRABGRASS A SECOND DOSE OF CRABGRASS PREVENTER.
About one month after your first treatment, apply a second to stop the seeds that survived the first treatment from germinating.

6. RINSE OUT YOUR SPREADER EVERY TIME, ESPECIALLY AFTER USING FERTILIZER.
Fertilizer is essentially a type of salt. And it eats up any metal parts it finds.

7. AERATE IN THE FALL IF YOU HAVE HEAVY LOAM OR CLAY SOIL.
(No need if you have sand.) Just before you fertilize, rent an aerator and aerate the lawn from both directions. It will help loosen the soil and allow the fertilizer to penetrate deep into the soil.

8. GIVE YOUR LAWN A GOOD FLAT-TOP FOR WINTER.
Just this one time each year, set your lawn mower to 1-1/2 to 2 in. and clip it off. That'll help retard mold during the winter.

9. WATER NEW SEED LIGHTLY AND TWICE A DAY OR MORE.
If you don't bother keeping the soil moist over new seed, don't bother seeding. Dampen the soil even more often during hot, windy weather. Keep watering for at least two weeks and don't miss any days.

10. RAKE UP DOWNED LEAVES IN THE FALL.
Those soggy leaves will suffocate the new sprouts in the spring and leave dead spots all over your lawn.

11. CHOOSE "SLOW-RELEASE" FERTILIZERS.
Rather than feeding the lawn all at once, this type allows the lawn to snack over a longer period. These fertilizers cost a bit more but are well worth the added expense.

12. DON'T APPLY TOO MUCH SEED.
You should try to achieve a concentration of about 15 seeds per square inch. If you exceed this, you'll have an overpopulated lawn with too many plants competing for nutrients and sunlight.

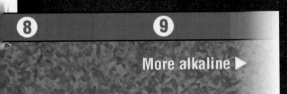

8   9

More alkaline ▶

5 TIPS FOR DEALING WITH LEAVES

Expert advice for fall foliage

YOU'VE PROBABLY BEEN RAKING LEAVES since you were a kid. And you might figure that there's nothing left to learn. That's what we thought too. But when we asked The Family Handyman's crew of Field Editors for advice, we got this heap of tips for saving time and labor. Take a few minutes to read the following pages to save yourself hours of work this fall.

4. A Tarp Beats a Trailer

Instead of bagging or hauling leaves, I rake them onto a tarp, which I drag into the woods. It's even easier if you get your kids to do it!

5. Vacuum in Tight Spots

A leaf blower/vacuum sucks up leaves fast, especially around shrubs, in flower beds and in other hard-to-rake areas. You might think that the bag would need to be emptied every five minutes, but the vac minces the leaves and packs a mountain of them into just a few bags.

1. Rake Picks

Lots of Field Editors told us about their favorite rakes. The most popular rakes are beloved just for their size—a big rake makes the job smaller. Most home centers carry rakes up to 30 in. wide. Other Field Editors swear by "no-clog" rakes—the tines don't skewer leaves, so you don't have to stop and unclog the rake. Several manufacturers make them, also in widths up to 30 in.

2. Bag 'em

We have a BIG yard and lots of trees. So I bag the leaves with my mower. It does a nice job of shredding the leaves, so they're ready to become compost or mulch.

3. Mulch 'Em

A mulching mower shreds leaves into tiny flakes that settle into the turf and decompose into natural fertilizer. You might have to go over some areas two or three times to completely chop up the leaves. Still, it's fast and easy and it makes the grass happy.

CHAPTER 6

HOME SAFETY

CHOOSE FIRE-RESISTANT SIDING

If you're installing new siding, install Class A-rated fire-resistant materials such as metal, fiber cement shingles and clapboards, and masonry. Using these materials can reduce your premium by up to 20%, especially in dry areas of the country that are more susceptible to fire damage.

Throw Burglars a Curve

A great way to thwart criminals is to trick them at their own game. Studious thieves will actually learn how to dismantle different types of security systems. So, while you want to communicate to burglars that you have a security system, you don't want to give away which one is installed. For that reason, put out a yard sign and window decals that don't match the system you have in your home. You can buy a variety of security signs and stickers online.

Outdoor sensor inside your house

Remote Temperature Monitoring

Have a second home that you visit seasonally? Here's a way to make sure all is running well—if you have a neighbor whose willing to keep an eye on the place. To make it easy on them, use electric timers to trigger lamps so they can see that the electricity is on. Also, get a wireless temperature station that has an outside sensor and an indoor display panel. When you leave, put the outdoor sensor inside your house and ask your neighbor to put the display panel on their kitchen counter. Instead of going out into the cold to make sure the furnace is OK, all they have to do is look at the indoor reader to see what the temperature is inside your house. Works well!

Display panel on neighbor's kitchen counter

STAY-CLOSED PATIO UMBRELLA

Some strong winds can blow your patio umbrella out of its stand and send it flying. The wind gets under the umbrella and opens it, making it take off like a kite. Besides damage to the umbrella, it could soar into a window or cause damage elsewhere. Here's a way to keep the umbrella closed and in its stand: Get a dog's quick-release collar and wrap it around the umbrella. It's a perfect fit! Find a collar at your local pet store.

SAFER SAW FENCE

Cutting small parts on a miter saw is dangerous. There's typically a wide gap between the fence halves and another gap in the throat plate. Without full support for the workpiece, small offcuts can (and will) go airborne. To solve this problem, attach a sacrificial fence.

Make the fence by gluing and nailing a length of 1x4 to a piece of 1/4-in. plywood. Attach the 1x4 to your saw's fence. Miter saw fences usually have holes predrilled, but if yours doesn't, just drill a few. Two holes on each fence section is sufficient. The fence greatly increases safety and makes it super easy to get accurate cuts. After you've made one cut, the kerf tells you exactly where your saw will cut. Just mark a cutting line on your workpiece and line it up with the kerf.

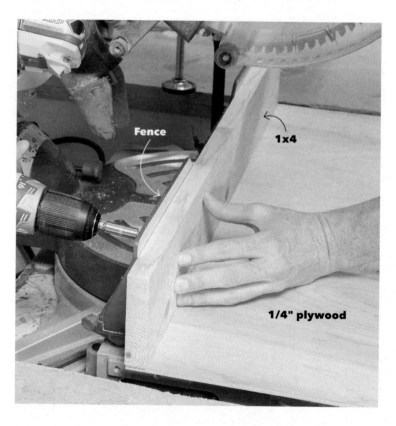

Fence

1x4

1/4" plywood

Mailbox Alert

In bad weather, no one wants to walk down a long driveway to see whether the mail has come yet (especially if it hasn't). A driveway wireless alert system is a great solution.

Mount the sensor module in the back of the mailbox and the receiver module in your living room. When the mailman opens the mailbox door, inserts the mail and closes the door, the chime will go off. No more unnecessary trips.

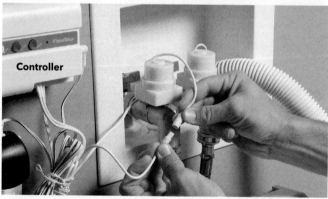

Controller

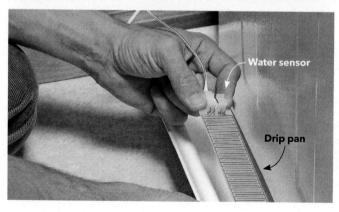

Water sensor

Drip pan

Avoid Flooding Disasters

Flooding from washing machines happens more often than you think. The machine's water valve, drain hose and pump can fail and cause major damage. This is especially concerning if your machine is on an upper floor.

A washing machine valve shutoff kit puts all that worry to rest. When the floor-mounted sensor detects puddling, it instantly shuts off the water valve.

The unit installs quickly with a slip-joint pliers. All you have to do is turn off the water and remove the fill hoses from the valves. Install the new motorized valves (**photo top**). Then mount the controller close to the nearest electrical receptacle and connect the wires (**photo middle**). Place the water sensor below the machine (**photo bottom**).

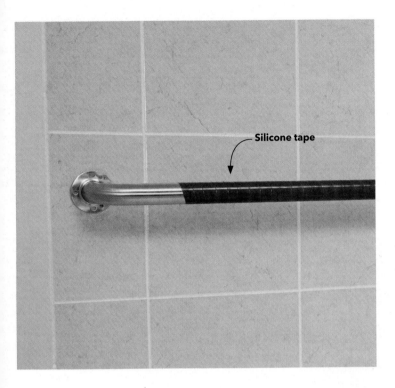

Silicone tape

NONSLIP GRAB BAR

Sometimes the grab bars in a shower can get a little slippery. One quick fix is to wrap them with Stretch & Seal silicone tape. It grips well and stays where you put it. Just be sure to stretch it as you wrap it so it sticks to itself. You can also use it to get a better grip on lots of other handles.

WHERE TO KEEP FIRE EXTINGUISHERS

Common sense dictates that you should keep fire extinguishers wherever there's potential for an accidental fire, such as in kitchens and garages. But some fire experts also recommend keeping them in places like laundry rooms and workshops and at the tops of basement stairwells. Extinguishers should never be more than 75 ft. away from a Class A (ordinary combustibles) hazard and no more than 50 ft. from a Class B (flammable liquids) hazard. When you mount a fire extinguisher to a wall, keep it high enough so kids can't reach it, near an exit and away from any kind of heat source. Also, place extinguishers a safe distance from items and areas with the highest risk for fire so you can get to one when you need it most.

DIY SNOW BLOWER CHUTE CLEANOUT

To prevent hand injuries, new snow blowers come with a cleanout device for clearing a plugged chute. If you own an older snow blower, retrofit it with your own cleanout tool. Just screw a pair of broom spring clips to your snow blower and snap in an old broom cut to size. You'll have the tool handy when your chute plugs, and you can brush all the snow off your snow blower before you put it away.

Spring
clip

Old garden hose

Outdoor Cable Protection

If your cable and telephone lines are left exposed along the foundation of the house, you could accidentally nick them with a weed trimmer or lawn mower. A slick trick for protecting the cables is to slit a section of old garden hose and wrap it around the exposed cable. Bury the end of the hose in the ground and whack away at your weeds.

Slip-Proof Wood Steps

Before winter hits, apply a coat of paint and traction grit on slippery wood steps. Sand and aluminum oxide grit are cheap, but both require constant stirring, and they show up as dark specks as soon as the paint starts to wear. Instead, try polymeric plastic grit (such as Seal-Krete Clear Grip), available at home centers. Polymeric grit stays suspended in the paint as you apply it, and because it's clear plastic, it won't show up as dark specks when the paint wears.

If you want grit that's easier on bare feet, add rubber grit to the paint (such as SoftSand Rubber Texturizing Particles). Use the broadcast method shown to apply it.

TRAVEL-SIZE ICE MELT

For small areas, don't lug around a big bag or bucket of deicer. Instead, save a Parmesan cheese canister and fill it with the deicer. With its large holes for shaking out product, the canister makes a perfect dispenser.

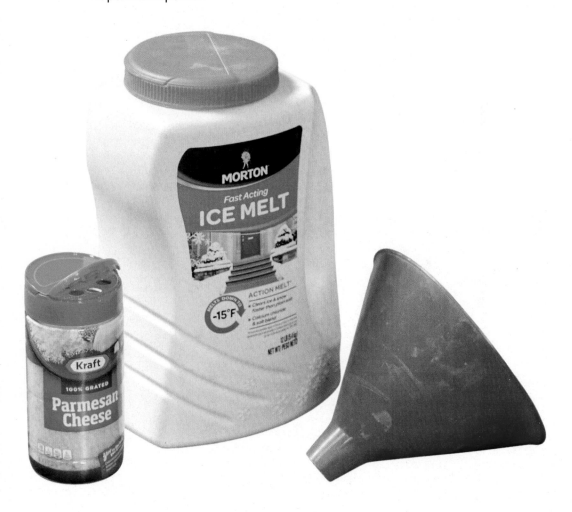

5 STEPS TO SECURE A HOME

Most crooks avoid challenges. They just want a quick, easy score.

UNDERSTAND YOUR FOES. Most burglaries occur on weekdays between 10 a.m. and 5 p.m. The perpetrators are usually substance abusers in their twenties looking for easy-to-pawn items to raise quick cash. They look for homes that appear unoccupied during the day, are dark at night, display signs of wealth (such as expensive cars and fancy decks), and are shielded by fences or shrubbery. And they always prefer breaking in through a ground-level side window or back door.

Most burglars don't pick locks or break glass. That takes too long, makes noise and risks personal injury. Instead, they simply kick in a door (even doors with a dead bolt) or pry open a window or sliding patio door. In many cases, they take advantage of a homeowner's carelessness by climbing in through an open window or unlocked door (window screens and storm doors offer no protection). Burglars tend to shy away from homes with dogs and homes with an alarm system.

Once inside, burglars head right to the master bedroom looking for gold jewelry, cash, furs and guns. Next, they scoop up prescription drugs from the bathroom and finish up with laptops, tablets and smartphones. Then they hightail it out.

Your job is to make your home less of a target, frustrate their attempts to break in and limit your losses if they do attempt to get inside.

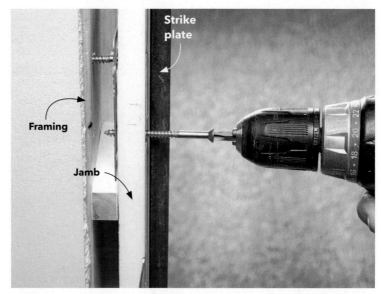

1 **Strengthen the doorjamb.** Remove the puny 3/4-in. screws from the strike plate. Drill pilot holes into the framing behind the jamb. Then drive in 3-in. screws to anchor the strike plate to the framing.

1. REINFORCE YOUR EXTERIOR DOORS

Burglars can open most entry doors with a few kicks or body blows. Even with a dead bolt, a blow shatters the doorjamb and splits the door itself (even steel doors). You can dramatically increase the strength of your doorjamb by installing longer strike plate screws that anchor into the stud behind the jamb (**photo 1**).

The first step would be to take out one of the existing screws. If it's shorter than 3 in., replace it. For even greater doorjamb security, consider installing a 6-in.-long heavy-duty strike plate (about $15). This is a much bigger job because you have to mortise a larger opening and drive in six 3-in. screws. However, if your entry door butts up to a sidelight and you can't install long screws, buy and install a 48-in.-long doorjamb reinforcement plate.

Next, prevent door splitting with a door edge guard. Measure the door thickness and dead bolt lock backset before you head to the home center. Then buy a guard (about $25) to fit around your door and dead bolt. Installing the guard takes about 15 minutes (**photo 2**).

2 **Install an edge guard.** It will keep the door from splitting from a sudden blow. Simply remove the dead bolt and screw on the guard.

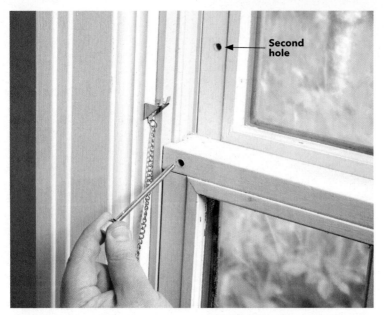

Second hole

Secure double-hung windows. Add a pin lock to prevent the sash from being pried up. Drill a hole to lock the window closed, and a second hole a few inches up to lock the window partly open for ventilation.

2. STRENGTHEN WINDOWS

The factory latches on double-hung windows are no match for a burglar with a pry bar. But thieves can't get past inexpensive pin locks (about $4 each). You can install a pin in just a few minutes per window (**photo left**).

Pry bars work on casement or sliding windows too. But the pin lock we show here won't work with them. Find casement and sliding window locks for about $5 per window at home centers.

3. SECURE SLIDING PATIO DOORS

There are two ways a burglar can easily get past sliding patio doors: by prying the door up and off the bottom track and by prying against the jamb and breaking the latch. To prevent latch breakage, some homeowners lay a long stick (like a broom handle) in the lower track. But a crook can easily move the stick with a coat hanger.

The best solution is to install a tension-fit drop-down security bar (aka "charley bar") and snap latch (**photo 1**). They're ugly, but they work and send a strong signal to crooks that you've fortified your home. To prevent the crook from prying the door up, install anti-jacking screws (**photo 2**).

1 Install a security bar. Secure the pivoting end of the security bar to the door frame at mid-height, so it's easy to operate and the crooks can see it. Then install the locking latch on the sliding door. Lower the bar and extend it so it wedges against the sliding door.

2 Install anti-jacking screws. Drive two 3-in.-long screws through the top track and into the header above the sliding door or window. Leave enough clearance to allow the sliding door or window to move, but not enough to allow a burglar to raise the door off the track.

4. LIGHT UP THE NIGHT

A well-lit home is your best protection against in-home assault and burglary. Light up all the vulnerable areas of your house and yard with dusk-to-dawn lighting (**photo above**).

It costs less than $4 per month to run four low-wattage CFL or LED floodlights all night long. If you have a motion sensor floodlight, swap in a photocell for just $15 (**figure below**). Or buy a ready-to-install dusk-to-dawn floodlight fixture for about $30 at any home center. Screw in cold-weather outdoor-rated floodlights and aim them at areas around your doors, windows and garage, and toward the alley.

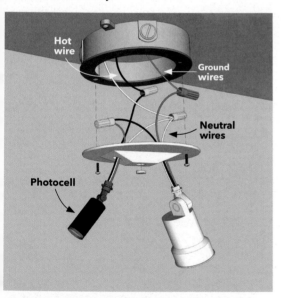

Hot wire

Ground wires

Neutral wires

Photocell

Turn off the power and double-check with a voltage sniffer. Then swap out the motion sensor with a photoelectric cell. Connect all the white neutral wires together. Then connect the black wire from the photocell to the black hot wire. Connect the red wire from the photocell to the light.

Alarm Systems Are Easier to Install Than You Think

Police interviews with burglars prove that alarm systems are a deterrent. If burglars are convinced your home has a real alarm system, they'll move on to a more vulnerable target rather than take a risk at your home.

You can buy a professional-grade wireless alarm system for about $200 to $400 from many online sources (homesecuritystore.com is one). Installing professional alarm hardware is easy, but programming the system can be a challenge.

For more information on installing a professional security system, go to familyhandyman.com and search for "security system."

However, if you don't want to tackle the programming or can't find a supplier who will program it for you, skip the professional gear and buy a consumer-style DIY wireless alarm instead. Starter kits come with a control unit, arming station, motion sensor and a few door/window sensors (**photo above**). But plan on buying enough extra sensors to install on each ground-level door and window.

Mount the arming station in a location where a burglar can see it from the most likely entry door or window. Then mount the sensors, connect the control box to power and your internet router, and program the system from your home computer. The system notifies you of a break-in or system failure with text messages and phone calls.

5. ADD VIDEO SURVEILLANCE, REAL OR FAKE

Burglars are increasingly aware that they're being watched, so a video camera can be a deterrent. A real video camera with good resolution costs about $300. However, you can get the same deterrent value by modifying a fake $20 camera so it looks real (**photo top**). Find fake cameras at home centers and online. Skip the smoked glass "dome" style and get a more traditional-looking unit. Mount it near the vulnerable doors and windows, but don't activate the red flashing light—real cameras don't have lights. Add coaxial cables to make it look real (**photo bottom**).

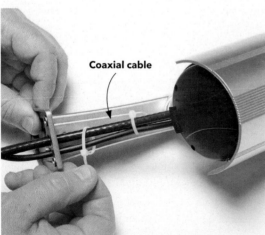

Coaxial cable

Make a fake camera look real. Real cameras have coaxial cables, so zip-tie coaxial cable to the fake power cable that came with the camera. Drill a second hole in the mounting bracket and hot-glue the cable into place.

Cut Your Losses If They Do Get In

- Immediately file a fraud alert with credit bureaus, and contact your bank and credit card companies.
- Inspect your checkbook for missing checks—close the account if any are missing.
- Don't keep cash in your bedroom.
- Get a nice-looking jewelry box and fill it with your less expensive jewelry. Keep your valuable jewelry elsewhere.
- Keep guns locked in a safe.
- If you haven't taken steps to secure your home since the burglary, do it now! Burglars often come back about six weeks later to get the brand-new items you bought with the insurance proceeds.